From the White House Inkwell

It is a grand place to live, but causes much work, some of which is impossible to do!

Harry Truman
July 18, 1963

Frontispiece: A TRUMAN White House engraving.

From the White House Inkwell

AMERICAN PRESIDENTIAL AUTOGRAPHS

JOHN M. TAYLOR

CHARLES E. TUTTLE COMPANY: PUBLISHERS

Rutland, Vermont

Representatives
Continental Europe: BOXERBOOKS, INC., Zurich
British Isles: PRENTICE-HALL INTERNATIONAL, INC., London
Australasia: PAUL FLESCH & CO., PTY. LTD., Melbourne
Canada: M.G. HURTIG LTD., Edmonton

Published by the Charles E. Tuttle Company, Inc.
of Rutland, Vermont & Tokyo, Japan
with editorial offices at
Suido 1-chome, 2-6, Bunkyo-ku, Tokyo, Japan

Book Plan by Roland A. Mulhauser

Library of Congress Catalog Card No. 68-29543

PRINTED IN JAPAN

FOR PRISCILLA

Contents

Foreword

FOR SOME TIME, the author has been impressed with the vast library of specialized works on various fields of philately. Entire books have been written on the stamps of a particular country, on certain types of cancellations, and even on a single issue of some particularly interesting denomination. The literature in the field of coin collecting is perhaps less voluminous than for philately, but it is nevertheless impressive.

With all due respect to *Manuscripts* magazine —the fine quarterly journal of The Manuscript Society—the paucity of specialized literature on autographs is rather remarkable. To be sure, there are many more philatelists than autograph collectors. But there must be at least the same market for a book on letters of the presidents, or of great musicians, or of signers of the Declaration of Independence, as there is for a book on "The US 3¢ 1851."

To date, books on autographs have generally fallen into one of two categories. One comprises books by autograph dealers, works which range in quality from fair to quite good. Inevitably, however, these are written from the point of view of the dealer. He is a fair and disinterested appraiser of autograph values, the final authority on the authenticity of any item, and in general a cultural pillar of his community. But for all this, it must be said that lay authors have given the dealers little competition. The second category of books on autographs, those by enthusiastic collectors, have had little to commend them to the general reader.

In this volume I have written about the most popular single field in American autographs, the Presidents. No explanation is required for the widespread interest in a field which represents, by its very nature, a history of the United States. In the chapters which follow, I have attempted to provide the reader with some idea of the relative scarcity of certain types of presidential autographs, and some idea of what a collector should expect to pay for them. This volume is not designed as a price guide, however, and the figures employed are meant to be approximate.

For the benefit of the non-collector, the term "autograph" as here employed refers not to a signature, but, in Webster's definition, to anything "which is written in one's own hand," i.e., any form of letter, document, photograph, or frank which incorporates someone's handwriting. An "Autograph Letter Signed," abbreviated ALS, is a letter entirely in the handwriting of the writer, and in theory is the most desirable form of autograph. Similarly, an LS is a letter signed but not written by the person concerned. The same distinction applies to documents, which may be an ADS, such as a check, or a DS, as with a commission.

At a time when autograph catalogs tend increasingly toward extravagant references to the "rarity" of certain presidents, it is worth noting at the outset that there are no "rare" presidents in the White House series. Several individuals are rare in ALS, and others are rare in letters written while in office. But one of the advantages in collecting Presidents is that autographs of all thirty-five are obtainable, albeit at a price.

The chain of events that has caused this book on American Presidents to be completed while stationed in the Republic of Singapore has made it impossible for me to invite comment on this manuscript from a number of persons whose views I would welcome. In the absence of such criticism, I am indebted to Mr. Robert Black, a dealer of many years' standing, for his replies to several questions concerning presidential documents.

For a volume in which the plates take on a special importance, I have been assisted greatly by librarians and collectors alike. Members of the staff of the Library of Congress —particularly Mrs. Dorothy Eaton and Mr. John Knoulton — were of great assistance in my search for presidential letters suitable for reproduction. I am indebted also to Dr. Herbert Klingelhofer Mr. Paul C. Richards and Mr. Bart Cox for providing me with facsimiles of presidential items from their own fine collections. Unless otherwise credited, all of the autographs shown in this volume are from the author's collection.

I wish particularly to acknowledge the invaluable assistance of my wife Priscilla, who not only shares my interest in American history but who supplements her knowledge with an ability to spell.

Finally, I am grateful to the following for their permission to quote from the works cited: World Publishing Company, *Personal Memoirs* by U. S. Grant; the Rutgers University Press, *Collected Works of Abraham Lincoln*; Barnes & Noble, Inc., *Zachary Taylor* by Brainard Dyer; Dodd, Mead & Company, *Grover Cleveland* by Allan Nevins; *Foreign Affairs* magazine, "The Historian and History" by Arthur M. Schlesinger, Jr.; Harper & Row, Inc., *In The Days of McKinley* by Margaret Leach; Houghton Mifflin Company, *Autobiography* by Charles Francis Adams, Jr.; the University of Oklahoma Press, *Collecting Autographs and Manuscripts* by Charles Hamilton; William Morrow & Company, *On Growing Up* by Herbert Hoover; Doubleday & Company, *John Adams* by Page Smith; Follett Publishing Company, *Treasury of Presidential Quotations* edited by C. T. Harnsburger; Charles Scribner's Sons, *The Presidency* by William H. Taft and *George Washington: First In Peace* by J. A. Carroll and M. W. Ashworth; Random House, Inc., *Life and Selected Writings of Thomas Jefferson* edited by Adrienne Koch and William Peden; Mr. Charles P. Taft, *The Life and Times of William Howard Taft* by Henry Pringle; Mrs. Faith McAdoo Haddad, "The Courtship of Woodrow Wilson" as printed in *American Heritage* magazine; Mr. Harry Barnard, *Rutherford B. Hayes and His America* by Mr. Barnard; Mr. Oliver Jensen, "The Gettysburg Address in Eisenhowerese," as printed in *Parodies: An Anthology*; The Macmillan Company, *Masks In v Pageant* and *Autobiography* by William Allen White, *The Available Man* by Andrew Sinclair, and The *Roosevelt Family of Sagmore Hill* by Herman Hegedorn; Alfred A. Knopf, *John Quincy Adams and the Union* by Samuel F. Bemis, and *The Vintage Mencken* edited by Alistair Cooke.

JOHN M. TAYLOR

CHAPTER ONE

President Washington

WHEN GEORGE WASHINGTON stepped down as President of the United States in 1797, Abigail Adams, wife of his successor, wrote of Washington, "He resigns the important trusts committed to him, covered with glory and crowned with laurels which will place him in the archives of time with the first of heroes and greatest of benefactors to mankind. . . . Take his character together, and we shall not look upon his like again." In view of the somewhat austere image of Washington which has come down to this generation of his countrymen, it is worthwhile recalling the pre-eminent position which he enjoyed among his contemporaries. He was truly first in war, and first in peace.

It would be unusual indeed if letters of Washington, the architect of the first great revolution of modern times, were not among the most sought-after of American autographs. And so they are, despite the fact that Washington's letters were rarely as intimate as those of many of his presidential successors. One of Washington's biographers has noted that "it was not Washington's habit to write often or fully on problems beyond immediate control."[1] In short, Washington's letters generally lack the philosophical content which often mark those of Jefferson and Adams. Yet the historical changes which Washington so profoundly influenced are of such import that the literary quality or lack thereof in his letters becomes irrelevant.

Washington's handwriting is one of the most distinctive of any president. As a young man, he wrote a tall, vaguely immature hand which bore little resemblance to the flowing, regular lines, so often compared to copperplate, which marched across his paper in later life. Once the transition was complete, there was little variation either in Washington's holograph or his famous signature.

Washington's correspondence was prodigious, and, even allowing for the quantity of his letters now in institutions, his autograph is not uncommon. Probably the most sought-after are letters dating from the Revolution, which as a group are more dramatic than those of his later career. This is the one period when Washington made extensive use of secretaries, who included at various times such luminaries as Alexander Hamilton and John Laurens.

If Washington's wartime letters are among his most interesting, they are also among his most gloomy. This is hardly surprising, for the situation of his army was seldom one to inspire good cheer. As early as 1776, however, Washington thanked a relative for taking an interest in his western lands, adding that "in the worst event they will serve for an asylum." At about the same time, during the siege of Boston, he wrote,

The reflection on my situation and that of this Army produces many an unhappy hour when all around me are wrapped in sleep. Few people know the predicament we are in on a thousand accounts; still fewer will believe, if any disaster happens to these lines, from what cause it flows. I have often thought how much happier I should have been, if, instead of accepting a command under such circumstances, I had taken my musket on my shoulder and entered the ranks, or if I could have justified the measure

The discharge of a Revolutionary soldier, signed by WASHINGTON.

No 16.   Philadelphia March 3: 1793.

Gentlemen,

This will be handed to you by Docter Thornton of this City, who goes forward to lay before you a plan which he has prepared for the Capitol proposed to be built in the Federal City. — Grandeur, Simplicity and Convenience appear to be so well combined in this plan of Docter Thornton's, that I have no doubt of its meeting with that approbation from you, which I have given it upon an attentive inspection, and which it has received from all those who have seen it and are considered as judges of such things. —

How far the expense of such a building, as is exhibited by the plan, will comport with the funds of the City, you will be the best judges, after having made an estimate of the quantity of materials and labour to be employed in executing it. — And to obviate objections that may be raised on this head, it should be considered, that the external of the building will be the only immediate expense to be incurred. — The internal work — and many of the ornamental parts without, may be finished gradually, as the means will permit, and still the whole be completed within the time contemplated by law for the use of the building. —

With very great esteem,

I am, Gentlemen,

Your most Obedt. Servant

G. Washington

The Commissioners of
the Federal District

33

A presidential LS of WASHINGTON, in which he strongly endorses architect William Thornton's design for the present U. S. Capital. (Library of Congress)

to posterity and my own conscience, had retired to the back country, and lived in a wigwam.[2]

Although Washington employed his secretaries for most official correspondence, most private matters he handled himself, including supervision of his estate at Mount Vernon and adjustments to his famous dentures. The latter consisted of pieces of ivory set in wood, the upper and lower sections held in place not by suction but by a spring. His dentures occasioned Washington much anguish, and go far in explaining the unsmiling portraits of the First President which have come down through the years.

Because of the heavy demand for Washington's letters, he has proved a favorite subject for forgers. Fortunately, his handwriting is difficult to imitate, much more so than that of Lincoln, the other president whose popularity has tempted the forger. The most frequently encountered Washington forgeries are holograph checks. These are skillfully done, but the writing is usually smaller than that of the subject, and when closely examined betrays a lack of rhythm which is uncharacteristic of Washington.[2]

It is the author's impression that the forging of autograph letters may be a vanishing art. The problems entailed in obtaining the "right" paper and ink, to say nothing of mastering the subject's handwriting, appear to deter would-be forgers, although many old forgeries continue in circulation. A more serious threat today is that a collector may purchase in good faith authentic material pilfered from some institution.

Of the letters written by Washington during his two presidential terms, many concern personal matters, especially real estate, and others relate to applicants for office. In a letter to Patrick Henry, however, Washington hinted in 1795 at the substance of his subsequent Farewell Address:

My ardent desire is, and my aim has been . . . to comply strictly with *all* our engagements, foreign and domestic; but to keep the U States free from *political* connections with *every* other Country; to see that they *may be* independent of *all* and under the influence of *none*. In a word, I want an *American* character, that the powers of Europe may be convinced we act for *ourselves* and not for *others*.[3]

Among the most interesting letters which date from this period are some which Washington drafted for his wife Martha. In marked contrast to Abigail Adams, Martha did not write letters easily. In an apparent attempt to ease her correspondence chores, Washington, who had more

than enough letter-writing of his own, took to drafting letters for his wife. These letters, which Martha duly copied and signed, permitted Washington some humorous references which are all the more amusing when one recalls that they appeared to come from his wife. In one letter he/she wrote,

I am now, by desire of the General, to add a few words on his behalf, which he desired may be expressed in the terms following, that is, to say—that disparing *[sic.]* of hearing what may be said of him, if he should really go off in an apopletic fit or any other fit . . . he is glad to hear before hand what will be said of him on that occasion; conceiving that nothing extra will happen between this and then, to make a change in his character—for better or for worse—and besides he has entered into an engagement with Mr. Morris and several other Gentlemen not to quitt the theatre of this world before the year 1800. . . .[4]

As will be noted from this quotation, Washington's spelling and punctuation were, in the manner of the day, subject to whim. His autographs are found in many forms. The pre-Revolutionary Washington is represented by land surveys executed in his late teens, by various financial documents and vouchers, and occasional letters, the latter being somewhat scarce from this early period. Land surveys by the young Washington used to be fairly common, but now command prices in four figures.

Among his later autographs are a variety of wartime letters and documents. These will run anywhere from around $600 for a routine circular letter to several thousand dollars for a letter of particular importance. Although these are usually LS rather than ALS, their content is such that they generally command higher prices than does a routine postwar ALS. Washington did not sign a great many presidential documents by comparison to his successors, and such as are available usually run $400 and up. A particularly desirable form of Washington's pre-presidential documents is the Revolutionary discharge, a certificate which acknowledged service by a soldier of the Continental armies and entitled him to public land. With rare exceptions, these were personally signed by Washington.

One group of intriguing Washington autographs derives from a crime against history.

Philadelphia Decr 25th 1793.

Dear Sir,

Your favor of the 18th inst. enclosing a statement of sales of lots in Roxburgh, belonging to us, has been duly received; and I thank you for the particular manner in which they a[...]made. —— I did not mean to give you so much trouble; to know summarily what had been sold and what remained on hand, was all I had in view. ——

I hereby acknowledge the receipt of a Bank note (New York) for Sixteen hundred and fifty nine 50/100 dollars being the Bal^e of y^r acc^t stated on the sales above mentioned

~~I offer you the compliments~~

Mrs Washington joins me in offering you, Mrs Clinton & family the compliments of the season & the return of many, many (happy) of them —— with great & sincere ~~regard~~ (friendship)

I am —— Dear Sir,

Y^o most Ob^t & affec^t Servt

G^o Washington

His Ex^y
Govr Clinton

An ALS to Governor Clinton in the famous WASHINGTON hand. Note the substitution of "friendship" for "regard" in the final line of text. (Library of Congress)

Before leaving the White House, Washington drafted a farewell address which he subsequently discarded in favor of the version which incorporated language provided by Hamilton and Madison. The earlier draft found its way to Jared Sparks, President of Harvard and an early biographer of Washington. Sparks was periodically asked for examples of Washington's autograph, and to oblige them he divided Washington's address into brief fragments without ever having made a true copy! Although sections of the manuscript appear from time to time, it has never been possible to reconstruct the address in its entirety. One is tempted to say that history is too serious a business to be left to historians.

CHAPTER TWO

Early Presidential Documents

ON MARCH 9, 1797, President John Adams bemoaned some of the responsibilities of the office he had just assumed. To his wife Abigail he wrote,

> To reconcile yourself to your fate, I have a great mind to give you a detail of mine. A peck of troubles in a large bundle of papers, often in a handwriting almost illegible, comes every day from the office of ——, office of ——, office of ——, &c., &c., &c. Thousands of sea letters, Mediterranean passes, and commissions and patents to sign.

What annoyed Adams was to become a widely denounced presidential chore, the signing of official documents. Over the decades, there would be sporadic efforts to reduce the number of papers requiring the president's personal signature. Yet the documents so roundly denounced by our second president are today assiduously sought by collectors of autographs and early Americana as artifacts of our beginnings as a nation.

In any discussion of presidential letters, one need only make a few elementary distinctions as to classification, i.e., ALS vs. LS. On the other hand, there are a number of varieties of presidential documents, and only one of those cited by John Adams—the presidential commission—is still in use today. The autographs of many of our early presidents are far more common on documents than in letters. With respect to our modern presidents the reverse is true, and most of them are more easily obtained in letter form than in documents. There follows a discussion of those presidential documents most frequently encountered, starting with the more common types.

First of all, there were land grants. From the administrations of Washington through the first term of Andrew Jackson, grants of land by the government, acquired either as compensation for military service or through purchase, were certified by a vellum deed signed by the president. Until the formation of a Land Office during Madison's administration, land grants were also signed by the Secretary of State, and the most sought-after grants are those signed by Washington and Jefferson.

Although many collectors view land grants as a rather lowly form of autograph, it should be noted that those of our first three presidents are by no means common. Not until after the Louisiana Purchase became available for distribution did land grants truly proliferate, but beginning with Madison such grants are common. The collector should be extremely wary of any grant purportedly signed by a president after Jackson, for these were almost invariably signed in the president's name by a secretary, as, indeed, were those of Jackson during his second term.

A second type of presidential document comprised commissions and appointments. In terms of format, there are numerous variations, but each serves to commission an individual to a post or military rank. Those of civil officials tended to be on paper as opposed to vellum and were relatively plain. Those of military and naval officers included ornate designs; depending on the service, they featured helmets, flags and cannon balls or nymphs cavorting among the waves. The design of such commissions changed little through the years, and they make most attractive display pieces. They went out at the time of World War I, however, and such commissions signed by Wilson are comparatively scarce.

Another decorative item was the ship's paper, sometimes called a sea letter or, in the case of certain ones, a Mediterranean pass. These appeared in several different formats from the time of Washington to that of Lincoln. Signed by both the President and the Secretary of State, they authorized the ship in question to clear its port of departure, and asked officials of the various countries to be visited to extend courtesies and necessary assistance. Some of these papers were double folio size, on paper, and in four languages. Others were smaller, on vellum, with engraved nautical vignettes at the top. Listing as they did a ship's cargo, and often its ports of call, ship's papers exuded a tang of the sea. They are understandably among the most sought-after of presidential documents.

A ship's paper was a type of document that was almost always signed in blank, the pertinent details being filled in later. Clearly, if a ship was about to sail from New Bedford, there was no time to send a paper to Washington, rout the President and Secretary of State out of bed, and return the signed paper to Massachusetts. Because of the prevailing practice of keeping a stack of ship's papers on hand at major ports, there are instances in which such papers have been filled in and issued after the president who signed it had died or left office!

Along with land grants, particularly those dispensing several thousand acres, that form of document most appreciated by the original recipient was the presidential pardon. These were signed by the President and Secretary of State, and usually embodied a cheerful little description of the crime for which a pardon was being granted. Larceny of varying forms was a frequent subject for clemency; pardons for capital crimes were less easily procured. Signed pardons, as opposed to warrants authorizing a pardon, which

are discussed elsewhere, are quite scarce. In contrast to various forms of commissions, few pardons were ever framed by their recipients.

Among the scarcest forms of presidential documents are letters patent and proclamations. Until Jackson's second term, each patented improvement was attested to by the President, the Secretary of State and the Attorney General. To these papers was attached a detailed description of the invention in question, sometimes complete with drawings. Here, as with all documents requiring the signature of the Secretary of State as well as the President, there are desirable two-president combinations. Perhaps the most sought after are pairings which include Thomas Jefferson, himself an inventor of note. But of all the patents registered in Washington, D.C., the most autographically famous is doubtless No. 6469. Granted in 1849, it provided means for buoying riverboats over shoals by means of inflated cylinders. The inventor was one A. Lincoln.

Even scarcer than patents are signed presidential proclamations and executive orders. The latter are not unlike proclamations, but generally are directed only to government departments. Presidential proclamations can be classified as either emergency or ceremonial, although the Emancipation Proclamation, of which Lincoln signed a number of souvenir copies, could be regarded as either one. There are a number of signed copies of the proclamation in which President Coolidge decreed a day of mourning for the late President Harding. Mr. Truman has signed souvenir copies of certain of his proclamations, including that of V-J Day. Typed copies of a proclamation, usually signed at a later date, are of course not the same as the real article.

Proclamations, like the various forms of commissions, have been employed throughout our history. Next to the Emancipation Proclamation, perhaps the one of greatest renown is that of George Washington who, on October 3, 1789, did "recommend and assign Thursday, the 26th of November next, to be devoted by the People of these States to the service of that great & glorious Being who is the benificent Author of all the good that was, that is, or that will be."

A final type of presidential document, one not easily defined, is the warrant, sometimes called the seal authorization. An Act of Congress passed in 1790 empowered the Secretary of State to place the Seal of the United States on signed presidential commissions, but stated that for the seal to be placed on any other instrument a special warrant was required. From that time until the administration of Harry Truman, presidential warrants were employed to authorize a variety of executive actions. The wording of the warrant, unchanged through the years, read, "I hereby authorize and direct the Secretary of State to affix the seal of the United States to . . . dated this day, and signed by me: and for so doing this shall be his warrant."

Warrants are to be found in many autograph collections today, but the Presidents are by no means uniformly represented. The earliest president whose warrant I can recall is Andrew Jackson; the latest is McKinley. Thus many Presidents are unobtainable in warrants. By way of contrast, there seems to be a limitless supply of warrants of Johnson, Grant and Hayes.

The explanation appears to lie in the manner in which warrants came into the autograph market. Around 1912 the State Department cleaned out many of its files in what is now the Executive Office Building next door to the White House. Quantities of dead files were taken into the courtyard and burned, among them a great number of old warrants. The sight of so many presidential signatures appears to have stimulated the curiosity of some of the clerks, who retrieved a few handfuls of the documents as souvenirs. The fact that these were rescued more or less at random accounts for the prevalence of certain names in warrants while others are not represented at all.

Not long ago it was fashionable for serious collectors to look down upon presidential documents as little more than signatures—unless, of course, the document in question happened to be a Lincoln commission promoting General Grant. This is no longer the case. Certain documents, particularly commissions and ships' papers, are increasingly appreciated as very striking display pieces. Many a warrant is associated with a treaty or other major event of American history. In the pages that follow, due notice will be taken of the availability of the various Presidents in documentary as well as letter form.

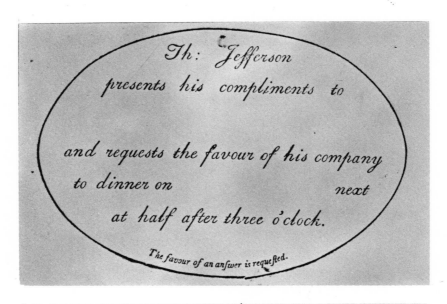

JEFFERSON's invitation card. On the reverse he has penned
the arrival and departure times of stages to Charlottesville.
(Library of Congress)

CHAPTER THREE

Thomas Jefferson

IF WASHINGTON WAS the indispensable man of the battlefield, Thomas Jefferson was the philosophical father of the Revolution. While it may be argued that Washington's was the more important contribution, the fact remains that their talents were very much complementary. As the commander of an amateur army, and more often than not badly served, Washington was inevitably the pragmatist. As one who articulated the goals and values of the modern world's first great revolution, Jefferson operated on a very different plane.

Jefferson, like most mortals, was prone to founder when outside his chosen environment. As a wartime governor he was ineffective, in part because his concepts of limited government were inadquate to a military emergency. Nor did politics bring out the best in Jefferson, and his acquiescence in the harsh attacks on Washington by Republican journalists does him little credit. Yet those who contend that the pen is more powerful than the sword can point to no better example than Jefferson. After Ben Franklin, Jefferson was probably the most influential American of his day. For decades Jefferson articulated the ideals of American democracy, and set his stamp not only on his own two terms as president but on those of his two successors as well.

The correspondence of Jefferson, like that of Lincoln, is of such a magnitude and of such importance as to resist brief commentary. No American president has relied more on the written word for propagation of his gospel than did Jefferson, and not until Lincoln did any match his eloquence. Many of Jefferson's letters were, in effect, essays on government designed to be read by many persons other than the original recipient. But he could also draw a dramatic word picture, as in this description of Paris in 1787:

> The mobs have ceased; perhaps this may be partly owing to the absence of parliament . . . the Queen, going to the theatre at Versailles with Madame de Polignac, was received with a general hiss. The King, long in the habit of drowning his cares in wine, plunges deeper and deeper. The Queen cries, but sins on. . . .[5]

Considering that he eventually was to take office under America's new Constitution, it is interesting to recall that Jefferson's initial reactions to it were by no means enthusiastic. "How do you like our new constitution?" he was asked by John Adams in November of 1787. "I confess there are some things in it which stagger all my disposition to subscribe to what such an assembly proposed. The house of federal representatives [Congress] will not be adequate to the management of affairs, either foreign of federal. Their President seems a bad edition of a Polish King."

As time went on, and Jefferson heard of the proposed Bill of Rights, he became less critical. He shortly took office as Washington's Secretary of State, a position which at that time embraced a variety of responsibilities in addition to those involving foreign relations. Jefferson's unquenchable intellectual curiosity is nowhere better illustrated than in his letter to one Eli Whitney, who claimed in his patent application to have a new device for processing cotton:

As the state of Virginia, of which I am, carries on household manufactures of cotton to a great extent, and as I do myself, and one of our great embarrassments is the clearing the cotton of the seed, I feel a considerable interest in the success of your invention for family use. Permit me therefore to ask information from you on these points. Has the machine been thoroughly tried in the ginning of cotton,

Respected Sir   Monticello June 24. 26

The kind invitation I recieve from you on the part of the citizens of the city of Washington, to be present with them at their celebration of the 50th anniversary of American independance; as one of the surviving signers of an instrument, pregnant with our own, and the fate of the world, is most flattering to myself, and heightened by the honorable accompaniment proposed for the comfort of such a journey. it adds sensibly to the sufferings of sickness, to be deprived by it of a personal participation in the rejoicings of that day. but acquiescence is a duty, under circumstances not placed among those we are permitted to controul. I should indeed, with peculiar delight, have met and exchanged there, congratulations personally, with the small band, the remnant of that host of worthies, who joined with us, on that day, in the bold and doubtful election we were to make, for our country, between submission, or the sword; and to have enjoyed with them the consolatory fact that our fellow citizens, after half a century of experience and prosperity, continue to approve the choice we made. may it be to the world what I believe it will be, (to some parts sooner, to others later, but finally to all,) the Signal of arrousing men to burst the chains, under which monkish ignorance and superstition had persuaded them to bind themselves, and to assume the blessings & security of self government. that form which we have substituted restores the free right to the unbounded exercise of reason and freedom of opinion. all eyes are opened, or opening to the rights of man. the general spread of the light of science has already laid open to every view the palpable truth that the mass of mankind has not been born, with saddles on their backs, nor a favored few booted and spurred, ready to ride them legitimately, by the grace of god. these are grounds of hope for others. for ourselves let the annual return of this day, for ever refresh our recollections of these rights, and an undiminished devotion to them.

Continued on next page.

I ask permission here to express the pleasure with which
I should have met my ancient neighbors of the City of Washington
and of it's vicinities, with whom I passed so many years of a
pleasing social intercourse; an intercourse which so much re-
-lieved the anxieties of the public cares, and left impressions so deeply
engraved in my affections, as never to be
forgotten. with my regret that ill health forbids me the gratification
of an acceptance, be pleased to recieve for yourself and those for whom
you write the assurance of my highest respect and friendly attachments.

Th: Jefferson

One of JEFFERSON's last letters. In it he regrets not being able to attend ceremonies commemorating the Fiftieth Anniversary of the signing of the Declaration of Independence, ceremonies that fell on the day when both Jefferson and John Adams died. (Library of Congress)

Th: Jefferson presents his compliments to Col°. Wor-
-thington, & incloses a draught of a section; which he pro-
-posed to Genl. Smith to add by way of amendment to
the Volunteer bill. knowing Col°. Worthington to be friendly
to this important measure, he has taken this liberty, as
he had with Genl Smith that of delivering him the original.

A third-person ATS of JEFFERSON. Although undated, its contents indicate that it was written during his presidency.

or is it yet but a machine of theory? What quantity of cotton has it cleaned on an average of several days, & by how many hands? What will be the cost of one of them made to be worked by hand? Favorable answers to these questions would induce me to engage one of them. . . .[6]

Jefferson infused a literary quality into his letters which few American presidents ever matched. But not the least interesting characteristic of Jefferson's letters is the script itself. Jefferson's handwriting tended to be small and rounded; it changed remarkably little during his lifetime. The most curious thing about it was Jefferson's reluctance to use a capital letter at the beginning of a sentence. I do not know that Jefferson himself ever explained this peculiar manifestation of his egalitarian philosophy.

Jefferson's autographs, like those of Washington, are in no sense rare, despite the large number which have been absorbed by libraries and other institutions. Demand for Jefferson is such, however, that he is one of the most expensive of the presidents. The briefest ALS will generally run at least $350, and those with fine content and greater length will run into the thousands. In short communications Jefferson was prone to write in the third person, e.g. "Th: Jefferson presents his compliments . . ." and because these are generally regarded by collectors as less desirable than those in the usual first-person format, examples can be obtained for about $300. While he was resident in France, Jefferson wrote a considerable number of letters in French, in which he was fluent, and he sent some of his official letters to Washington in cypher.

Jefferson is well represented in LS, though these are not as common as his ALS. The bulk of his LS date from his period as Minister to France and Secretary of State, and in terms of content are often as fine as all except the most interesting of his ALS.

Fortunately, Jefferson is well represented in terms of presidential documents. A land grant can be obtained for around $150, although those which are countersigned by Madison are seldom found for less than $200. Ships papers and patents are still more expensive, as are acts of Congress attested to by Jefferson as Secretary of State. Jefferson's franks are prized by philatelists, and those as President are particularly desirable. In contrast to those of Washington, Jefferson's presidential franks generally incorporated his signature in full, e.g., "Th: Jefferson, Pr U. States."

Two qualities that stand out in Jefferson's correspondence are his attention to detail and his sense of history, if one may employ this overworked term. With respect to detail, Jefferson's letters reflect the same attention to specifics that marks his *Autobiography* and the *Notes on Virginia*. He was never too busy, even as President, to attend to the most minute affairs concerning his beloved Monticello.

As for the sense of history, no president except perhaps Lincoln had a keener eye for readers in future generations. This is reflected through much of his famous correspondence with John Adams. In contrast to Adams' straightforward outpourings, often affectionate, occasionally emotional, Jefferson is reserved and correct. He was quite capable of writing what his correspondent wished to hear, with the result that Alexander Hamilton emerges from the correspondence roughly on a par with the devil and Benedict Arnold. But Jefferson knew that he lived in momentous times, and no president's letters have contributed more to the historical record. Wrote Jefferson:

The letters of a person, especially of one whose business has been chiefly transacted by letters, forms the only full and genuine journal of his life; and few can let them go out of their hand while they live. A life written after these hoards become opened to investigation must supercede any previous one.[7]

CHAPTER FOUR

The Two Adamses

IN THE SPRING OF 1785, Elbridge Gerry wrote to John Adams to inform him that he had been chosen by Congress to be the first American ambassador to the Court of St. James. In passing, Gerry mentioned in some detail the debate which had preceded his selection, in which the New Englander had come under strong attack for his "weak passion," vanity. Properly indignant, Adams sat down and replied to Gerry with what amounted to an essay on vanity and its various manifestations. "According to all that I have read," wrote Adams, "there are, in mankind, various kinds of vanity, and every gradation of the passions." Adams thereupon analyzed various forms of vanity, coming to the conclusion that he was free of these particular strains. Finally, he observed that there was a form of vanity which, though it might be considered a weakness, derived from the testimony of a good conscience. "When a man is conscious of services and exertions from the purest principles of virtue and benevolence," and sees his labors "crowned with transcendent success, there arises a satisfaction and sometimes a transport which he would be very wise indeed if he can at all times conceal."[8]

If this exchange demonstrates nothing else, it demonstrates that the second president was a rather formidable correspondent, not disposed to the use of post cards. But to the generations of both John Adams and John Quincy, letter writing was the primary means of communicating over any distance; a vital chore, and not one to be taken lightly. Within the Adams family, so often separated by diplomatic assignments and other public business, the task of letter writing was developed into an art form.

The most remarkable of John Adams' correspondence is probably that with his wife Abigail, followed by that with Thomas Jefferson. Adams' biographer has written,

[Adams] and his wife provided a kind of counterpoise for each other. When Abigail was inclined to doubt that man was ever made to enjoy the delights of freedom John assured her that a wise and beneficent God would not have foreclosed that possibility, and when John was tempted to despair of the capacity of Americans for republican government Abigail expressed her faith that Americans had a special "character trait. Though sometimes misled and deceived, they wish to know what is just and right, and to conduct accordingly. In the thirty years of my life, in which I have attentively observed them," she wrote, "I have always found them returning to the right path, as soon as they have had time to weigh, consider, and reflect."[9]

The most striking characteristic of John Adams' letters is their emotional content. He held strong views on most subjects, and was all but incapable of dissimulation or evasion. In times of stress, he was prone to alternate between elation and melancholy, and all of this is reflected in his correspondence. In a dark period of the Revolution Adams wrote, "We have not men fit for the times. We are deficient in genius, in education, in travel, in fortune, in everything." Yet he was equally capable of exhilarating optimism, as in his letter to Abigail following the proclamation of American independence:

The second day of July, 1776, [sic.] will be the most

A presidential ALS of JOHN ADAMS, with his characteristic bold signature. (Library of Congress)

memorable Epocha, in the history of America. I am apt to believe that it will be celebrated, by succeeding generations, as the great anniversary festival. It ought to be commemorated as the day of deliverance, by solemn acts of devotion to God Almighty. It ought to be solemnized with pomp and parade, with shews, games, sports, guns, bells, bonfires, and illuminations from one end of this continent to the other from this time forward forever more.[10]

Philadelphia December 5: 1797

Gentlemen   No. 60.

I here enclose you, a Power to borrow 150,000 Dollars for the Use of the federal City, wherever you can find it.

If this Resource should fail of having its compleat Effect, I agree fully with you in opinion, that it will be necessary for your board to lay the whole Subject before Congress for their consideration and further provision and that it will be necessary for One of you to attend in Philadelphia, in order to explain all things to the Members of Congress. I have no Objection to the form you have prepared, and shall be ready to convey it by a Message to both Houses. I am with great Esteem Gentlemen, your most humble Servant

John Adams

Commissioners
of the federal City.

116

An ALS concerning finances for the new capital "federal city" of Washington. For most of JOHN ADAMS' term the capital was Philadelphia. (Library of Congress)

Quincy May. 15. 1815

Dear Doctor

I thank you for your favour of the 10th and the Pamphlet inclosed "American Unitarianism". I have turned over its Leaves, and found nothing that was not familiarly known to me

In the preface Unitarianism is represented as only thirty years old in New England. I can testify as a Witness to its old Age. Sixty five years ago, my own Minister the Reverend Lemuel Briant, Dr Jonathan Mayhew of the West Church in Boston, The Reverend Mr Shute of Hingham The Reverend John Brown of Cohasset, and perhaps equal to all, if not above all, The Reverend Mr Gay of Hingham; were Unitarians. Among the Laity, how many could I name Lawyers, Physicians, Tradesmen, Farmers.? I could fill a Sheet, but at present will name only one, Richard Cranch a Man who had Studied Divinity, and Jewish and Christian Antiquities more than any Clergyman now existing in New England

More than fifty years ago I read Dr Samuel Clark, Emlyn, and Dr Waterland. Do you expect, my dear Doctor to teach me any new thing in favour of Athanasianism?

There is, my dear Doctor, at present existing in the World a Church phylosophic as subtle as learned as hypocritical, as the holy roman, Catholic, apostolic and Œcumenical Church.

Continued on next page.

As is to be expected, Adams' is one of the most sought-after of presidential autographs. No president has surpassed and few have matched Adams' gift for interesting correspondence. Without seemingly attempting to, Adams was able to lend a touch of color to even the most

This phylosophical Church was originally English. Vol-
taire learned it from Lord Herbert, Hobbes Morgan Collins
Shaftsbury Bolingbroke &c &c &c

You may depend upon it your Exertions will promote
the Church phylosophie more than the Church Athenasian,
or Presbyterian.

This and the coming Age will not be ruled by
Inquisitions or Jesuits. The restoration of Napoleon, has been caused
by the Resurrection of Inquisitions and Jesuits.
I am, and wish to be your Friend
John Adams

Rev.d Dr Morse

A characteristically vigorous JOHN ADAMS letter, in a hand that begins to show the effects of age. (Library of Congress)

routine communications. His frequent absences from Abigail tended to make him irascible, and when irascible he wrote some of his most delightful letters.[11]

Adams was a prolific correspondent, probably even more so than Washington or Jefferson. Except while Ambassador to England, he penned moalst all of his own letters until the last decade of his life, when palsy forced him to employ secretaries. Despite their comparative abundance, it is difficult to find an Adams ALS for less than $300. Adams' handwriting varied so much at different times in his career that a novice collector, looking at two different ALS, will find it hard to believe that they are by the same person! During the period of his presidency, Adams' script, and especially his signature, reached its zenith in terms of size. His letters of this period often resemble the efforts of a child of about eight.

In contrast to many of his successors, presidential documents of Adams are not common, this despite his complaint, quoted earlier, concerning the time consumed in signing documents. One explanation for the scarcity is that Adams was a one-term president—the only one until John Quincy came along. Then again, as the President of a fledgling nation Adams had fewer ships to dispatch, and less land to give away, than did his successors. In any case, a good presidential document of Adams currently runs well over $200.

Other forms in which Adams' autograph is found include a variety of non-presidential documents. While Vice President, for instance, Adams was president of the American Academy of Arts and Sciences, and signed a number of membership certificates in that organization. Legal papers, dating from Adams' early days as an attorney, turn up fairly regularly. And among Adams' more interesting autographs are his franks. He had the franking privilege for much of his career, and to discourage misuse of his signature he generally franked between the lines of the address in a way which left no room for the forging of an I.O.U.

It is a remarkable thing that a democratic republic, in which election to high office generally requires a degree of popular appeal, elevated to the presidency so independent a spirit as John Adams. It is nothing short of astounding that the same democratic process saw the election of John Quincy Adams. One of John Quincy's biographers has related how an old man once came up to Adams, described how his wife had known the Adams family, and recalled how on occasion she had cut Adams' hair when John Quincy was a young boy. "Well," replied the President, with his customary warmth, "I suppose she cuts *yours* now."[12]

John Quincy was such a consummate un-politician that he could very probably have been elected only at the time when he was, and in the manner which he was. His election occurred at the end of Monroe's "era of good feeling" when there was a surge of nationalism that for a brief period obscured party divisions. Although Adams had no organized political following, neither did his rivals. On the basis of his distinguished record as a diplomat, and his distinguished lineage, Adams was the choice of 84 electors in 1824, at a time when presidential electors exercised their own discretion. But Andrew Jackson was the choice of 99 electors, and was the popular choice as well. Adams became president only after the inconclusive election went to the House of Representatives, where Henry Clay's followers chose to support the New Englander.

It seems fitting that old John Adams lived to see his son in the White House. In 1826, however, two days after he had participated in Fourth of July ceremonies in Washington, President John Quincy Adams received word that Jefferson had died on the holiday. "A strange and very striking coincidence," Adams noted in his journal. Two days later he received a letter advising that his father was failing rapidly, and the President had gotten as far as Baltimore en route to Quincy when he learned that John Adams, too, had died on the Fourth. "My father," wrote Adams, "had served to great and useful purpose his nation, his age, and his God." Like many of his countrymen, Adams was awed at the simulta-

London May 6th 1796.

My dear Brother

I have within these three days successively received your letters of the 17th and 28th of last month. I had previously grown extremely anxious on your account, not having heard from you for so long a time. My apprehensions were not without foundation, but from your last I am led to hope your recovery is by this time complete, and that the beauty of the season, will soon give you the strength which may still be deficient.

But your letter of the 22d mentioned in that of the 28th as containing an assignment for 200 guineas, has not yet come to hand. Its importance would at all times be considerable, but at the present it is of unusual magnitude to me, because the want of the supply with which it is to furnish me, is the only circumstance which still detains me here. I have received at length from America the letter which I have been expecting these four months, and am therefore more than ever impatient to take my departure. Had your letter of the 22d been equally fortunate with that of the 28th I should have improved personally the opportunity by which I now write.

I shall bring with me the articles of Mr. Niel, and the tooth brush &c for yourself. But you need not fit up or hire an house. I shall, however unwillingly, cross the water with no other companion beside my man Sancho.

You must get the news, from the papers I send.
your brother
J. Q. Adams.

T. B. Adams Esqr

An early letter of JOHN QUINCY ADAMS, written when he was 29. (Library of Congress)

neous passing of his father and Thomas Jefferson:

The time, the manner, the coincidence with the decease of Jefferson has the visible and palpable marks of divine favor, for which I would humble myself in great and silent adoration before the Ruler of the Universe. For myself, all that I dare to ask is that I may live the remnant of my days in a manner worthy of him from whom I came. . . .[13]

Lieut.ᵗ Thomas B. Adams — Fort Moultrie S. C.

Washington 1. Feb.ʸ 1831.

My dear Thomas.

Enclosed, you have a Blank Power of Attorney, to be filled up and executed by you to enable my Son Charles, to receive the Dividends upon the Stock standing in your name of the Suffolk Insurance Company at Boston — When executed, return it to me, and I will forward it to him — after which you will give him your directions for the disposal of the interest which may from time to time be received upon your funds at Boston —

There is a Resolution before the House of Representatives, the object of which is to discharge from the Army all the Supernumerary Officers, who after passing through the Academy at West-Point, have received Commissions by Brevet — In this number I think you are still included, and although it is doubtful whether the measure will be adopted at the present Session of Congress, you will do well to be thinking of what course of life you may find it expedient to adopt, in the event of your being disbanded — Should this event, contrary to my expectation take place the ensuing Spring, I invite you to come and spend it, and the succeeding Summer, with me, at Quincy, and in that time you will have leisure to look out for such other occupation as may be suitable to your interest and inclination.

We are here in our usual state of health, with an un-usually rigorous Winter — From the newspapers we gather that the late Snow-Storms which have ranged along the coast from North-Carolina to Maine have not reached your Station at Fort Moultrie — perhaps owing to an extra portion of Caloric in South Carolina.

Your affectionate Uncle   J. Q. Adams.

A post-presidential ALS of JOHN QUINCY ADAMS. In the last sentence he alludes to the nullification controversy in South Carolina.

John Quincy's autographic output was even more prodigious than that of his father. He appears to have spent an average of several hours a day on his correspondence, handling almost all of it by himself. On diplomatic assignments abroad, and while Secretary of State, Adams employed a secretary for some official communications, but except for these periods Adams' LS are hard to come by. Curiously, John Quincy Adams may have been the only president to have known and practiced shorthand. But this was of little help to him with his correspondence, as there is no record that he ever had a secretary who could read it!

Adams was not only the most dedicated diarist ever to occupy the White House, but he was also the most persistent poet. Although other Chief Magistrates may have taken poetic flights from time to time, John Quincy Adams was the only president to have published volumes of verse. Autograph poems by Adams come onto the market not infrequently, as do stanzas written into autograph albums. Full poems by Adams are quite desirable autographs, and often sell for $300 or more. This compares to the going price of around $125 for a routine Adams ALS.

In 1827, when Adams as President had yet to take a strong stand against slavery, he wrote in his journal on the anniversary of his father's birth,

Day of my father's birth, I hail thee yet.
　What though his body moulders in the grave,
　Yet shall not Death th' immortal soul enslave;
The sun is not extinct—his orb has set.
And where on earth's wide ball shall man be met,
　While time shall run, but from thy spirit brave
　Shall learn to grasp the boon his Maker gave,
And spurn the terror of a tyrant's threat?
Who but shall learn that freedom is the prize

Man still is bound to rescue or maintain;
That nature's God commands the slave to rise,
　And on the oppressor's head to break his chain.
Roll, years of promise, rapidly roll round,
Till not a slave shall on this earth be found.[14]

After Adams left the White House, and his anti-slavery convictions had become more pronounced, Adams caused the last two lines from this poem to be engraved on his father's tomb.

John Quincy Adams wrote in a small, rounded hand which was as regular as his father's was irregular. In terms of content, most collectors feel that John Quincy's letters lack the zest of his father's, but the younger Adams could nevertheless write a fierce letter when aroused, which was not infrequently. Except for his very early autographs, John Quincy's script tended to be quite palsied, particularly in his later years. Charles Francis Adams, Jr. recalled his grandfather as "An old man, absorbed in work and public life. He seemed to be always writing—as indeed, he was . . . a very old-looking gentleman, with a bald head and white fringe of hair—writing, writing—with a perpetual ink-stain on the forefinger and thumb of the right hand."[15]

John Quincy Adams is well represented in documents of virtually all types. There are passports dating from his period as Secretary of State, plus the usual run of presidential documents. His franks are abundant, and one occasionally encounters inscribed copies of his speeches or addresses in Congress. Adams does not appear to have developed a standard signature for documents, for some he signed in full and others as J. Q. Adams. Presidential documents of the second Adams generally run $45 and up.

CHAPTER FIVE

The Virginia Dynasty

WITH RESPECT TO our first three presidents, their elevation to the chief magistry was a logical sequel to their services to the nation during the Revolution. None of the three, in looking back on his political career, tended to view his election as president as the high spot of his service. Indeed, all of them at one time or another had second thoughts as to why a patriot should aspire to an office that carried with it such public abuse.

With the administrations of Madison and Monroe, however, there was a subtle shift in the popular attitude towards the presidency. No longer was it simply a matter of determining which Revolutionary leader was most deserving of the honor. As Jefferson's Democratic Republican party gained the political ascendancy, presidential aspirants, to have any hope of success, had to profess principles acceptable to the Jeffersonians. It was still expected that the electors would cast their ballots for citizens whose public careers merited the honor. But at the same time, the range of choice was increasingly circumscribed by factional and geographic considerations.

As the "Father of the Constitution" and a leading disciple of Jefferson, James Madison qualified on all counts. Of his predecessors, not even Washington had contributed more than he to the creation of the governmental structure of which the Executive branch was one part. In 1792 Madison had written to Washington,

We have established a common Government, which, being free in its principles, being founded in our own choice, being intended as the guardian of our common rights and the patron of our common interests, and wisely containing within itself a provision for its own amendment as experience may point out its errors, seems to promise everything that can be expected from such an institution; and if supported by wise counsels, by virtuous conduct, and by mutual and friendly allowances, must approach as near perfection as any human work can aspire, and nearer than any which the annals of mankind have recorded.[16]

Madison's letters tend to be straightforward and to the point, deriving their interest from the subject matter under discussion. They generally lack the philosophical content and historical allusions which make Jefferson's letters so memorable. Though Madison was not one to engage in personalities, his opposition to John Adams inspired Madison to write a letter in 1798 comparing the first and second presidents:

There never was perhaps a greater contrast between two characters than between those of [Adams] and his predecessor. . . . The one cool, considerate and cautious, the other headlong and kindled into flame by every spark that lights on his passions; the one ever scrutinizing into public opinion, and ready to follow where he could not lead it; the other insulting it by the most adverse sentiments and pursuits.[17]

Madison wrote this at a time when the Jeffersonians still idealized the "republican virtues" of the American electorate, and regarded the Executive as the servant of the electorate rather than its leader. In later generations, a president who "scrutinized into the public opinion" solely to follow its dictates would inspire little respect.

Nevertheless, Madison's ALS, once common, have become scarce in the last decade as more and more have been purchased by specialists. His earlier letters, including those as President, are

Washington July 21. 1812

D. Sir

I was duly favored with yours of the 8th. on the subject of the B. officer arrested near Norfolk. The circumstances which attracted your notice amply exposed him to suspicion; and it is more than possible that he had the views tho' not the full character of a Spy. It was thought best however to commence the war with an example of liberality, and he was permitted as a mere alien enemy to depart for his own country.

The papers inclosed contain specimens of the political Spirit which reigns at Boston; and of the manner in which a British Cabinet is made up.

accept assurances of my great esteem and friendly respects

James Madison

An ALS of MADISON, written during the War of 1812. The President explains that a certain alien was deported rather than tried as a spy, since it was "thought best . . . to commence the war with an example of liberality." (Library of Congress)

A rare MADISON document, signed as President of the American Colonization Society. The Society sought to resettle Negro slaves in Africa.

written in a neat, flowing hand devoid of ornamentation. He employed his full signature on official documents and letters, but in other correspondence frequently signed himself "J. Madison." In his later life Madison was increasingly troubled by rheumatism and his once-flowing script became irregular and broken. In his final years, Madison's holographs give the impression of having been shakily printed.

LS of Madison, like his ALS, are not common. As with Jefferson, the bulk of these date from his period as Secretary of State. A good LS of Madison will cost at least $150, the price having risen sharply as his ALS have become scarce. A full-page ALS is rarely found for less than $300, unless in the third person.

Fortunately for collectors, Madison documents are plentiful. The purchase of Louisiana by his predecessor stimulated something of a land boom, and it was left to Madison and Monroe to sign the grants. Madison is also well represented in ships' papers and military commissions, many of these countersigned by Monroe either as Secretary of State or Secretary of War. A document signed by both usually runs around $100 if in good condition, but a land grant by Madison alone can be obtained for around $50. Madison's franks, many of them executed as Secretary of State, are among the more common of the early presidents.

Among the presidents who preceded Andrew Jackson, only James Monroe regarded the presidency as the summit of his public career. By comparison to his predecessors, Monroe's pre-presidential accomplishments had been modest. He had been a captain in the Revolutionary army, and had been wounded at Trenton. He

Additional Instruction to the public and private armed vessels of the United States.

THE public and private armed vessels of the United States are not to interrupt any vessels belonging to citizens of the United States coming from British ports to the United States laden with British merchandize, in consequence of the alledged repeal of the British Orders in Council, but are on the contrary to give aid and assistance to the same; in order that such vessels and their cargoes may be dealt with on their arrival as may be decided by the competent authorities.

By command of the President of the United States of America,

Jas Monroe   *Secretary of State.*

WASHINGTON CITY, AUGUST 28, 1812.

A War of 1812 circular, signed by MONROE, that reflects the slow communications of the day.

Washington Dec. 4, 1819

Dear Sir

I have received your two favors of the 23d, and at the same time a copy of the revised code of the State, the value of which work, from my knowledge of the great talents & republican virtues of those employed in it, in succession, from the commencement of our revolution, I fully appreciate.

To the kind assurance of your friendship, I have a just sensibility, as it accords, with all my long standing impressions & feelings, in many relations. It will give me pleasure to promote the views of the young man mentioned, as in so doing, I shall, I am satisfied, render services to one having merit, while I meet the wishes of his estimable friends & advocates. On this subject I will write you again.

With great respect & esteem I am dear Sir sincerely yours.

James Monroe

A presidential ALS of MONROE. In it he praises the "great talents and republican virtues" of those responsible for the revision of a state's legal code.

"It is ready now for the cup and lips." MADISON sends
wine to a neighbor.

had studied law under Jefferson, after which he had entered Virginia politics. His "training" for the presidency might be said to have begun with his appointment by Washington as Minister to France. Monroe's diplomatic career was not wholly successful, however, and the pro-French bias which he exhibited while in Paris brought about his recall by Washington. In a letter written in 1809, Monroe complained that

It has been my poor fortune to be much harassed and calumniated let me serve under whom I may. It seems as if I can never get home after the discharge of important trusts abroad . . . in peace. My head must be pelted by the storm if I ever expose myself to it.[19]

Of the Presidents heretofore discussed, Monroe's autograph is by far the most common. Full ALS of Monroe, including examples as President, can be obtained for less than $150, and his documents, especially land grants, are extremely common. Monroe probably signed more two-president documents than any of his contem-

poraries. His signature as Secretary of State with Madison, however, is somewhat more common than those with himself as President and John Quincy Adams as Secretary of State.

Although nearly all our early presidents felt the financial pinch at times, none suffered more embarrassment than Monroe as a result of the government's failure to pay his claims. He also incurred losses in real estate, and a pathetic number of letters in his later years relate to his efforts to raise money to meet his debts. Considering Monroe's own difficulties, there is a special pathos in a letter which he wrote to Thomas Jefferson, sympathizing with his friend's financial difficulties:

I mentioned in a letter which I lately wrote to you, that I had seen in a paper from Richmond, a notice of an application which you had made to the legislature, for permission to sell a large portion of your estate, by lottery, for the payment of your debts. . . . I have been much concerned to find, that your devotion to the public service, for so great a length of time, and at so difficult an epoch should have had so distressing an effect, on your large private fortune. . . . It is a concern, in which I am satisfied, the people will take a very deep interest.[20]

Monroe wrote in a rough, angular hand which is generally legible but by no means aesthetic. He usually signed his name in full, but occasionally abbreviated his first name to "Jas." or, less frequently, used only the initial. His letters are generally straightforward, bristling with commas, and lacking in any special grace, but generally getting their point across. As such they were probably a fair reflection of their author. Monroe can be said to be the first president who "grew" to the responsibilities of his position. The one-time discredited diplomat eventually commanded the respect of all factions as President, and caused his two administrations to go down in the history books as the "era of good feeling."

CHAPTER SIX

The Jacksonians

THE ADMINISTRATIONS of Andrew Jackson and Martin Van Buren comprised, in a sense, a single political era. Throughout Jackson's two terms Van Buren was his companion, protege, and political spear-bearer. It is hardly surprising that Van Buren ended up as his mentor's political heir.

Their terms spanned twelve eventful years, during which the country surmounted the first threat of disunion, and the two-party system emerged in essentially the form which we know it today. For all their political kinship, however, two more different personalities could hardly be imagined than "Old Hickory" and "The Little Magician." Although Jackson was hardly the barbarian which his enemies were fond of portraying, he was nevertheless the survivor of numerous duels, a scourge of the plains Indian, and the instigator during Monroe's administration of a rash invasion of Spanish Florida. He was the first president to be born west of the Alleghenies and, in a clear break with the Tidewater tradition, the first born in that celebrated American institution, the log cabin. In short, Jackson was the incarnation of the frontier.

Consider then his protege, Van Buren. A graduate of Union College, Van Buren was a successful lawyer in central New York before entering Democratic politics. In Albany, at a tender age, he established one of the earliest and smoothest of political machines, the "Albany regency." He was a skilled propagandist, and observed while in Albany that without a newspaper run by "a sound, practicable and above all

discreet republican . . . we may all hang our harps on the willows."

An early disciple of Jackson, Van Buren worked hard on the General's campaigns, although the two never met until Jackson was President and had named the New Yorker as his Secretary of State. Relations between the incoming Democrats and the outgoing Adams administration were exceedingly bitter; yet in a gesture entirely in keeping with his instinctive courtesy, Van Buren was the one senior representative of the new administration who called on President Adams in the period preceding Jackson's inauguration.

As might be expected, the letters of Jackson and Van Buren reflect the differences in their temperaments—although Van Buren's temper was a good deal more even than his handwriting. Jackson's letters are straightforward, often blunt, and written in a rough, virile hand. In signing his name, he often appears to have been surprised at having reached the edge of the page; there is usually a contrast between the giant "A" of "Andrew" and the cramped final letters of his surname. Some of Jackson's finest letters were written at the time of the nullification controversy, in which South Carolina first posed the threat of a state's seceding from the Union. In one letter he wrote,

Nullification means insurrection and war. . . . Can anyone of common sense believe the absurdity that . . . a state has a right to secede and destroy this union and the liberty of our country with it, or nullify the laws of the union; then indeed is our constitution a rope of sand; under which I would not live.[21]

what the Duke might have expected or intended, I was satisfied with the assurances Mr. Vageot gave me, that he would immediately state what had occurred to his Government.

All which is respectfully submitted, with the hope, if the course pursued is approved by the President, that this report may be filed in this Department with the letters to which it refers.

Wm Forsyth

Approved.
Andrew Jackson

A presidential endorsement by ANDREW JACKSON, who approves action taken by his Secretary of State.

Jackson's letters are not particularly scarce, but demand is such that his is one of the more expensive presidential autographs. He is fairly easily obtained in ALS, although as President he employed a secretary for much of his correspondence. As noted earlier, Jackson was the first president to rebel against the number of documents requiring his signature, and during his second term virtually all land grants were signed by proxy.

Few presidents have written a better letter than Old Hickory. Just prior to his famous victory over the British at New Orleans Jackson had occasion to write, "I will hold New Orleans in spite of Urop and all hell" (which prompted Theodore Roosevelt to observe, nearly a century later, "If that doesn't spell Europe, what does it spell?"). But his letters to his wife Rachel were as tender as those to his enemies were brusque.

A Jackson ALS can rarely be obtained for less than $250, or an LS for less than around $150. There is no problem in obtaining items of presidential date, but many of his most interesting letters were written from retirement at The Hermitage. Presidential documents of Jackson have lately risen considerably in price. A ship's paper or patent will run between $75 and $100, and more if countersigned by Van Buren.

Jackson not only wrote a good letter, but inspired literary flights in others. One can well imagine the indignation which prompted John Quincy Adams, on hearing that Jackson was to be given an honorary degree by Harvard, to write in 1833, "I would not be present to see my

A JACKSON ALS, written just a few months before his death, in which he expresses apprehension concerning prospects for the administration of President Polk. (Library of Congress)

darling Harvard disgrace herself by conferring a Doctor's degree upon a barbarian and savage who could hardly spell his own name."[22]

In contrast to Jackson's letters, the bulk of Van

> Lindenwald
> Apl. 10th 1849

Gentlemen

    I feel myself honored by your invitation to attend the Festival to be given by the friends of Henry Clay on the occurrence of his Birth day.

    It affords me much pleasure to be assured of the favorable reception by your Association of the opinions I have heretofore expressed of the Character and claims to public Consideration of your venerable friend, & of the nature of your devotion to him. Those opinions are still entertained; and I therefore need only add an expression of my sincere regret that it will not be in my power to avail myself of your present politeness.

    I am, Gentlemen, very respectfully & truly yours

    M. Van Buren

To
Matthew L. Davis
Willis Hall & others
a Committee &c

VAN BUREN pays tribute to Henry Clay. The neat handwriting suggests either that it is an LS, or that Van Buren took unusual care with a letter that he thought would be read at the ceremonies.

Buren's tend to be verbose and uninspired in content. Moreover, Van Buren's handwriting is the worst of any president prior to John F. Kennedy. He could on occasion write a legible

A midshipman's warrant signed by VAN BUREN, approximately half size. Warrants were smaller and less ornate than the commissions given officers.

letter, usually for some ceremonial occasion at which the letter was to be read. Most of what he wrote, however, was in a free-running scrawl. A letter which Madison or Polk would have fitted into one page Van Buren could spin into three or four nearly-illegible sheets.

Van Buren's autograph is one of the most common among pre-Civil War presidents. He is moderately scarce in letters written during his single presidential term, but from his home in Kinderhook, N.Y., he carried on an extensive correspondence from the time he left office in 1841 until his death in 1862. He survived his term of office longer than any other president, and the abundance of his letters, combined with limited demand, has thus far kept prices low. An ALS of Van Buren can sometimes be obtained for as little as $30.

The absence of interesting Van Buren material

is somewhat surprising, for he, like many of his contemporaries, corresponded extensively concerning political matters of the day. Nor was he always the evasive "Little Magician" that his political enemies described. Van Buren's unwillingness to endorse the annexation of Texas, an unwillingness reflected in a series of important letters at the time, probably cost him his renomination by the Democrats in 1844. When the Civil War came, Van Buren was the only one of the living ex-presidents who supported the policies of the Lincoln administration.[23] Yet for all his public service, Van Buren remains something of an enigma. Perhaps this is because, among contemporaries who employed the bludgeon, Van Buren preferred the rapier. He was by no means the devious scoundrel described by his opponents, but he may well have been one of our first full-time politicians.

A military LS, embodying WILLIAM HENRY HARRISON's full signature. (Collection of Dr. Herbert Klingelhofer)

CHAPTER SEVEN

Tippecanoe and Tyler, Too

WHEN WILLIAM HENRY HARRISON died of "bilious fever" in the spring of 1841, he achieved two unenviable distinctions. Not only did he become the first president to die in office, but he set a record for brevity in the Executive office which has yet to be matched.

Until his election as president, fortune smiled on Harrison with some regularity. Few regarded him as a great soldier, but over a period of years he projected a martial aura even while soldiering on a part-time basis. A lackluster term as Congressman from Ohio, and a nearly disastrous tour as American Minister to Colombia, did not dim his political luster. He was nominated as the Whig candidate over a number of talented but less "available" aspirants, including the formidable Henry Clay, in a depression year which made victory over the incumbent Democrats a virtual certainty.

Harrison's significance in terms of autographs stems largely from the extreme rarity of his autograph while in office. To my knowledge, no one has attempted to identify and number such examples as exist. Persons with many years' experience in American autographs seem to agree that no more than two or three presidential letters of Harrison are known to exist. There are perhaps a dozen Harrison documents, including several ships' papers. Such documents invariably fetch four figures at auction, and a good letter would bring many times more.

Even in his pre-presidential period, Harrison's output in terms of letters was not great. His autograph would be quite scarce were it not for a large number of vouchers dating back to the years 1794–96 when he was aide to General Anthony Wayne. Although sniffed at by some collectors, these vouchers with which Harrison paid spies, reimbursed sutlers, and provided whiskey for innumerable Indian tribes are not without a certain charm. Some are DS, others ADS, and most are signed "Wm. H. Harrison."

Except for its rarity while in office, Harrison's is not a particularly interesting autograph. It is unusual to find a letter of good political content, although some of his letters during and after the War of 1812 have fairly good military content. Those from other periods often deal with real estate, legal matters, and routine military chores. These are sometimes quite long; it is perhaps significant that Harrison's inaugural address as President was the longest ever, even after some blue-penciling by Daniel Webster.

Harrison wrote a rough but legible hand. His signature varied somewhat during his lifetime. The early "Wm. H. Harrison" gave way to "Wm. Henry Harrison" as general and as governor of the Northwest Territory. Later on he favored simply his first two initials, and this is what is found on his autographs of presidential date. Harrison sometimes failed to date his letters, and one encounters certain ones dated enigmatically "Sunday," or not at all. Content and the law of averages, however, conspire to place these in the pre-presidential period.

It is ironic that Harrison's name is today irretrievably associated with an obscure skirmish at Tippecanoe, the significance of which was re-

A later ALS of HARRISON concerning financial matters. Although undated, it probably was written in the late 1830's.

membered, even in Harrison's lifetime, by few persons other than hard-working Whig songwriters. Whatever his ability as a commander, it was Harrison who in 1813 defeated the British and Indians at the Thames to restore American control of the Old West.

Although it is difficult to imagine Harrison's becoming one of the "great" presidents, there were those who saw his administration as full of promise. Col. Zachary Taylor wrote of the late President's cabinet in 1841,

I do not believe a purer, more talented & independent body of men could have been brought togather [sic.] or selected for the Stations they filled, or who had more at heart the interest & welfare of the country, & who in point of disinterestedness & every qualification I do not expect to see replaced during my time . . . but I will not despair of the republic let what come that may.[24]

Until fairly recently, Tyler ranked with Van Buren, Fillmore, and Cleveland as among the most common autographs of the nineteenth century presidents. Lately, there has been a resurgence of interest in Tyler, whose career touched so many of the great issues of his day, from the time he entered Congress in 1816 until he died in 1861 while a member-elect of the Confederate legislature.

Tyler is seldom ranked with the more important Chief Executives, yet his role in the history of the presidency is a significant one. As the first vice president to succeed to the presidency through the death of his predecessor, it was Tyler who set the precedent that the vice president shall succeed to the full powers of the presidential office and not merely be an "acting president." Later, Tyler became the first president to marry while in office.

This presidential letter to Henry Clay, chiding him as "too impetuous," is probably the finest HARRISON letter extant. As one of two or three known examples of his ALS as president, it would probably bring between $5,000 and $10,000 at auction. The doodling is in pencil, and could easily be removed. (Library of Congress)

Tyler tended to be a verbose penman, but curbed this tendency while in the White House. His letters while in office were generally quite direct and to the point. Certain of Tyler's letters

(18)-

Williamsburg January 7. 1841

My dear Sir;

Your very kind letter of the 2d Inst reached me by last mail, and in reply I have to return you my thanks for your invitation to take shelter under your roof in the event of the contemplated visit of the President elect, to the City of Richmond. I shall do so with the greatest plea-sure. My hope is that Genl Harrison will not permit any slight impediment to turn him aside from his expected visit to Virginia. The freeest interchange of feeling and sentiment with his friends in Richmond, and he has none more sincere any where, is particularly desirable before he shall have committed himself upon the subject of his Cabinet. Your estimate of the great importance of the first step is every way just, and I hazard nothing in saying that if his cabinet be cast of the proper ma-terial that from that moment the voice of faction will be entirely silenced as to his future course. The question of the succession is the one to be shunn'd as far as may be, in all its bearings.

With the assurance of my sincere regard
I am Dr Sir
Truly Yr
John Tyler

Gov. Gilmer

6389

Vice President–elect TYLER writes of a forthcoming visit by the President-elect. (Library of Congress)

come close to being ADS in the technical sense of the word, for he was prone to omit the formal salutation, and frequently dated letters following his signature. As did so many of his presidential

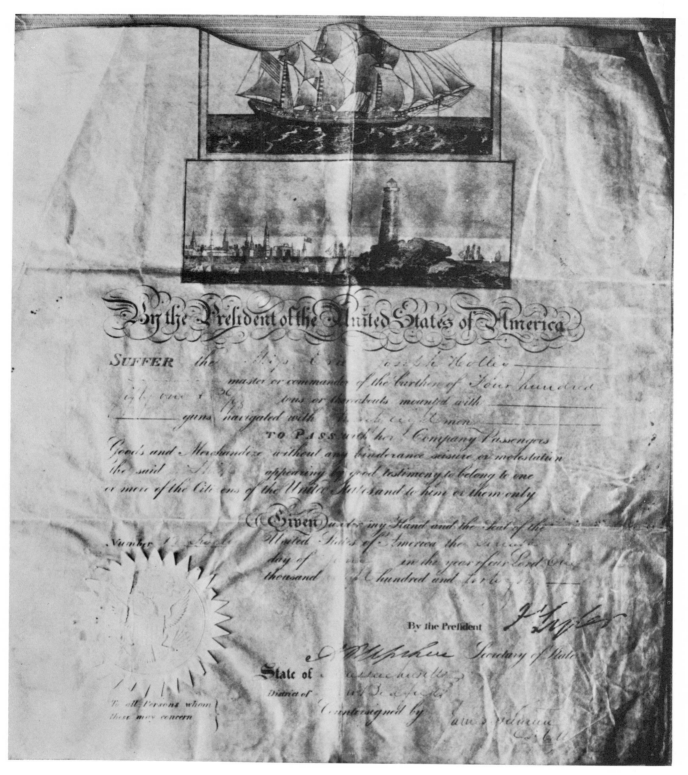

A ship's paper signed by President TYLER and countersigned "posthumously" by Secretary of State Abel P. Upshur. Although the document bears the date June 7, 1844, Upshur had died the previous February in an explosion aboard the U.S.S. "Princeton."

predecessors, Tyler handled almost all of his correspondence personally, and as a result LS of Tyler are rare indeed.

The same progression in the size of signature which characterized John Adams is noticeable with Tyler. As a congressman and senator, he wrote a small "John Tyler" with the signature hardly larger than the letter text. While in office his signature increased in size, with the first name generally dropped in favor of the initial. After leaving office, Tyler resumed the use of the full "John" and his signature diminished in size, but he added a small flourish, the obvious prerogative of an ex-president.

Although many of Tyler's letters contain an attractive turn of phrase, he did not write a large number of interesting letters. Tyler was the last of the early Virginia Dynasty to occupy the Executive Mansion, and much of his correspondence is that of the country squire, on subjects such as meeting a loan payment, doctoring the cow, and housing relatives. In this connection, it might be noted that Tyler was prolific in more than correspondence. Married twice, he was the father of 15 children, the last of whom died in 1947.

Tyler had a wry sense of humor that stood him in good stead throughout a career in which he frequently found himself at odds with his own Whig party. A political renegade, he named his Virginia estate Sherwood Forest. Years later, he penned this obituary for his horse:

Here lies the body of my good horse, "The General." For twenty years he bore me around the circuit of my practice, and all that time he never made a blunder. Would that his master could say the same![25]

CHAPTER EIGHT

Polk and Taylor

ONE EXPLANATION for the growing interest in presidential letters is their relative availability. The collector of Signers of the Declaration of Independence, however affluent, often must resign himself to an incomplete set, lacking Button Gwinnett and/or Thomas Lynch, Jr. There simply are not enough examples to go around. However, no such aura of defeatism inhibits the collector of Presidents. The budget-minded collector may have to settle for clipped signatures in a few instances, but the material is available for those who can handle the financing.

Thus it was noted earlier that none of the Presidents is a rarity in the sense that some famous Americans are. Among the major autographic rarities may be included Edgar Allen Poe, Herman Melville, Jesse James, Stephen Foster, and Daniel Boone. Having said this, however, it remains true that some Presidents are scarcer than others; moreover, certain Presidents (like Madison) are common in documents, but scarce in letters. Others, including most of the twentieth century presidents, are common in LS but very scarce in ALS.

Such fine points aside, two of the more scarce of the pre-Civil War Presidents are James K. Polk and Zachary Taylor. Over the years, fewer of their autographs, of all types, have come onto the market than of most of our nineteenth-century presidents. The reasons are not difficult to ascertain. Taylor died in office, while Polk survived his term by less than a year. Neither, obviously, carried on the voluminous post-White House correspondence of such figures as Van Buren and Tyler.

A second factor is that both Polk and Taylor were out of the public eye for much of their pre-presidential years. Taylor was an officer of the regular army, and spent much of his time at obscure frontier posts. Polk was a figure of some prominence in the Democratic Party, and he served a term as Governor of Tennessee and as Speaker of the U.S. House of Representatives, but was of such little prominence nationally that he is generally regarded as the first "dark horse" presidential nominee. Neither Polk nor Taylor appears to have impressed his contemporaries as a luminary whose correspondence should be carefully preserved. Their contemporaries instead treasured letters of Henry Clay and Daniel Webster.

Taylor, "Old Rough and Ready," wrote a heavy, masculine hand thoroughly in keeping with his nickname. In many of his letters the ink is so heavy that in places it has eaten through the paper. Taylor's correspondence tends to reflect his background as a soldier and a planter; much of it is related to routine military and financial affairs. The grammar is rarely stylish, yet he usually seemed able to get his message across. Years later, in his *Memoirs,* Ulysses S. Grant was to write,

Taylor was not a conversationalist, but on paper he could put his meaning so plainly that there could be no mistaking it. He knew how to express what he wanted to say in the fewest well-chosen words, but would not sacrifice meaning to the construction of "high-sounding" phrases. . . . Taylor was pleasant to serve with. . . . (He) saw for himself, and gave orders to meet the emergency without reference to how they would read in history.[26]

The Hon. J. R. Poinsett
Secretary of War   Washington City
                                        July 2nd 1838

                        Sir

                                In the event the Bill
now before Congress, — to increase the present
Military establishment of the U. States, should
become a law, the undersigned, take pleasure
in recommending — to your favourable consideration, Capt. Barton A. Wilds, of Tennessee, as
a person eminently qualified, for a Captaincy
in the New Regiment, provided for by the
Bill. — Capt. Wilds, commanded a company
of Tennessee Volunteers, under the immediate
command of Maj. Sanderson, in the late
Campaign in Florida. — Capt. W. refers to

Continued on next page.

Grant may have been overly charitable; a recent biographer of Taylor has observed that "The most serious threat to General Taylor's presidential chances was not from other candidates, but from his own pen."[27] As a hedge against indiscretion, most of Taylor's letters during the 1848 campaign, and subsequently in the White House, were written by secretaries,

An ALS of POLK recommending an Army officer, signed also by other Members of Congress from Tennessee.
(Courtesy of Paul C. Richards)

including his son-in-law, "Perfect" Bliss. This led to considerable improvement in the grammar, but also caused Taylor to become rare in presidential ALS. Among nineteenth century presidents, only the first Harrison, Garfield, and perhaps Johnson exceed Taylor in the rarity of their presidential ALS. A presidential ALS of Taylor would probably run around $500.

Neither Taylor's handwriting nor the form of his signature changed noticeably during his adult life. He always preferred to use the initial for his first name, and it is doubtful whether a full "Zachary" can be found outside of a legal docu-

ment. His signature is marked by the large size and copybook construction of the final "r."

In handwriting as in many other traits, James K. Polk was the antithesis of Taylor, whom he mistrusted, and whom he fought desperately and unsuccessfully to keep out of the White House. Polk wrote an attractive, somewhat embellished hand, and had the most ornate signature of any president. His elaborate paraph was and is the despair of forgers, as Polk probably intended that it should be. Yet one suspects that habit and exhibitionism also played a part. Even when Polk signed a short note with initials only, as he

Washington City 24th Octr 1845. —

My Dear Sir!

I was exceedingly gratified to receive to day, your letter of the 10th and Post Marked on the 16th Instant, inclosing the letter written to me by General Jackson on the 6th of June last, but two days before his death, and being as you informed me in a former letter, the last letter which he ever wrote to any one. — I return it above all price, and will preserve it as a Memorial of the friendship of the dying patriot, a friendship which had never been broken for a moment been broken from my early youth till the day of his death. — It breathes — the most ardent friendship for me personally, and for the success of my administration. The moment I learned from my friends in Tennessee, and from the Nashville Union, that such a letter had been written — and that it was the last from his pen, you knew the anxiety I felt to receive it. — Your explanation — of the manner in which it was by accident — thrown aside — with other papers on his table — in the midst of the confusion of the dying scene is

Continued on next page.

perfectly satisfactory, — and is as you will remember — precisely what I conjectured — in might have happened, in my letter to you, making inquiry concerning it. — The whole mystery which rested over its supposed loss — or miscarriage, is now solved and satisfactorily. — It is marked "Confidential", and the principal subject to which it relates is of a highly delicate and con-fidential character. — The suggestions which it conveys — are very important, — and shall as he desired them to be, remain locked in my own bosom. — It is most remarkable with what clearness — he retained his intellect to the close of life, — and with what interest he viewed every thing connected with his political principles and the welfare of his country. —

With you be so kind as to present the salutations of Mrs. Polk and myself to Mrs. Jackson, and believe me to be;

With Great Respect
Most Truly
Your friend
James K. Polk

Andrew Jackson Jr.
Hermitage
Tennessee

President POLK writes of his late mentor, Andrew Jackson. Polk's letters are probably the scarcest of any nineteenth century president. (Library of Congress)

Baton Rouge Louisana
January 5th/1848

Mr __ Shaw the bearer a young artist of much merit & great promise, has just completed a portrait of me, in which my family & friends consider he has been very happy in its execution; in which I fully agree as far as I am capable of judging.

From his Mr, S. intelligence, gentlemanly manners & bearing, I beg leave to recommend him to all patrons of the fine arts; and he carries with him not only high respect & esteem, but my best wishes for his attainment of fame & fortune in the pursuit of his noble profession

Z. Taylor.

An example of TAYLOR's rough script. (Library of Congress)

was prone to do, he was never in too great a hurry to include an abbreviated paraph.

Although the quality of Polk's letters as a whole is only fair, a number of these date from his presidency, and a fair number of these concern aspects of the Mexican War. Polk was one of the hardest workers ever to occupy the White House, and he followed closely all aspects of the war effort against Mexico. Like the two Adamses, Polk kept a diary, and the intensity with which the President went about his business is reflected in some of the entries:

The public have no idea of the constant accumulation of business requiring the President's attention. No president who performs his duty faithfully and conscientiously can have any leisure. If he entrusts the details and smaller matters to subordinates constant errors will occur. I prefer to supervise the whole operations of the Government myself rather than entrust the public business to subordinates, and this makes my duties very great.[28]

An ALS of Polk can sometimes be found for $150 or less, while presidential documents run around $75 and up. Polk's franks are among the rarest of the presidential series, and command high prices from philatelists.

An autograph curiosity. The slanting final line of text, and the fact that it touches the signature, indicate that TAYLOR affixed his signature in blank, and the text was filled in later.

Polk was the last President whose Secretary of State (in this case James Buchanan) also became President, though three other administrations separated those of Polk and Buchanan. Documents signed by Polk and Buchanan, encountered in the form of ships' papers and pardons, are a good deal more scarce than similar documents of the Virginia Dynasty.

Curiously, Taylor and Polk, though moderately scarce, are far from the most expensive of presidential autographs. Comparatively few collectors attempt to secure more than an example or two of each, and thus far there seems to have been enough to go around. Should specialist interest develop for either President, prices would be in for a drastic rise.

In connection with scarcity, it might be noted that autographs of most First Ladies are a great deal more difficult to obtain than those of their document-signing husbands. In no case is this characteristic more pronounced than in those of Mrs. Taylor and Mrs. Van Buren. The former survived President Taylor by only two years; the latter died long before her husband became President Van Buren. Both First Ladies are virtually unobtainable in autograph form.

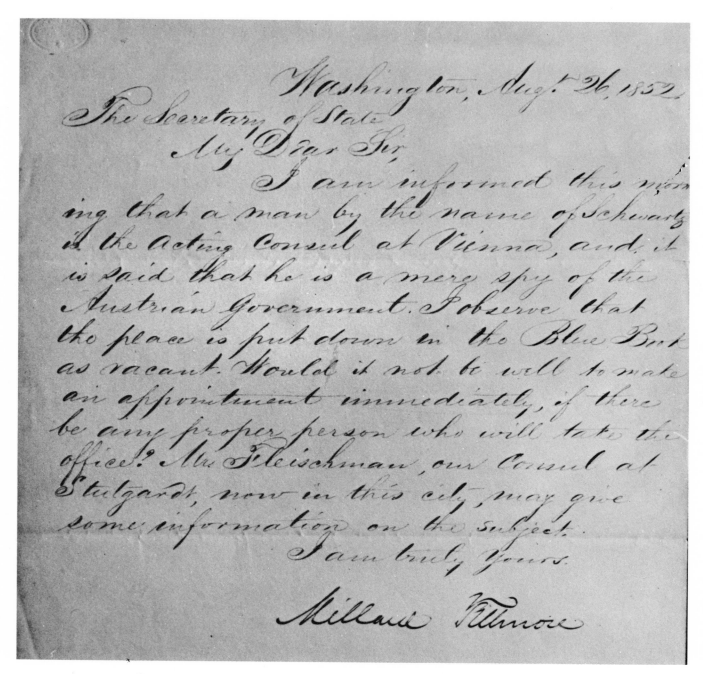

President FILLMORE, informed that one of his diplomatic officers is "a mere spy" of a foreign government, takes resolute counter-action in this LS to Secretary of State Daniel Webster.

CHAPTER NINE

Forgotten Men

A COMMENT SOMETIMES heard among American historians concerns the failure of the electorate, in the decade prior to the Civil War, to elect its leading statesmen to the presidency. Not only Webster and Clay, but also Douglas, Benton and Calhoun were passed over either by their parties or the voters. It is, of course, a truism that American political conventions usually seek to avoid any controversial choice when it comes to choosing a candidate. When this tendency led to the election of three rather nondescript presidents, Fillmore, Pierce, and Buchanan, during one of the critical periods of our history, it gave impetus to an interpretation of the Civil War as having been an unnecessary and avoidable crisis, brought on the country by a "blundering generation."

It is not necessary to refute this thesis at length to make the point that the three presidents in question, while hardly without faults, were more than mere blunderers. They were not persons of great imagination or perception, and at various times underestimated the depth of feeling in the nation concerning slavery and other sectional issues which contributed to the coming of the Civil War. They were, nevertheless, persons of integrity, devoted to the Union, who could hardly do other than to attempt to compromise the schisms which threatened to divide the country.

Millard Fillmore, who succeeded to the presidency when Taylor died, was an urbane political "pro," a self-made man who had risen from poverty to political prominence. However, he combined a conservative philosophy with a tendency toward pomposity which caused him to be regarded in some quarters as a bore, even in an era when wearisome oratory was the rule rather than the exception. Nevertheless, his administration has received an unduly harsh press at the hands of Northern historians. Many never forgave Fillmore for signing the Fugitive Slave Law in 1850, even though it was an integral part of the sectional compromise arranged by Henry Clay. Nor was Fillmore's reputation enhanced by his having run in 1852 as the candidate of the American "Know-Nothing" Party.

Autographically, Fillmore's letters are among the most common of any pre-Civil War President. Like Taylor, however, he used an amanuensis while in the White House, and his ALS as president are scarce, though not nearly as rare as those of his predecessor. Fillmore is credited with having installed the first bath tub in the White House. Almost as important, he organized the first White House library. A dedicated bibliophile, Fillmore amassed in retirement a large personal library which was scattered after his death. Volumes from his library, usually containing his signature and the date acquired on two different pages, are not difficult to come by.

Fillmore's letters, like the man, tend to be a bit on the dull side. They are carefully composed, however, and Fillmore's handwriting is among the more attractive of the presidential series. Fillmore is the first President of whom signed photographs are known to exist, though these

Washington March 10. 1851.

Dr Sir

The copy of the proceedings of a meeting of Whig Citizens of Philadelphia which you presented to me under date of 27th ult, I have to-day referred to the Secy. of the Treasury; and the request contained in them for certain changes in the Custom House in your city shall at a proper time receive due consideration.

This reference should have been made at an earlier day but for the circumstance that the papers got separated & have just been all collected.

Truly yours.

Millard Fillmore

Jn Stokes Esq
    Phila.

A scarce FILLMORE holograph as President.

                                    Concord Oct. 17, 1849

My dear Sir
                    Your letter of this date
has just been received — I am glad you
have seen your aunt and the other
persons as stated — I shall see you of course
at Manchester next week when I will give
you all necessary instructions as to witnesses
Your father should hold no conversation
either as to a settlement or reference — Marks
talk about a trial here & in relation to
your father, Robt & G is all perfectly
idle or as your mother properly
calls his extravagant & wild statements
"fabulous". Mr Ayer has given me
no notice, that more depositions will
be taken. And I of course shall not
go to Hills two Friday & Saturday
                    In haste
                                    yr friend & Servt
                                    Frank Pierce

Mr Lewis W. Alcock
        Allcock.
                    N.H.

FRANKLIN PIERCE, recently returned from Mexico, writes concerning a forthcoming law case. (Courtesy of Paul C. Richards)

date from his later years when he lived in Buffalo, N.Y. He enjoyed the franking privilege both as Congressman and ex-President, and his franks are among the most common of the

Concord N.H.
Oct 21, 1852

My dear Sir —
                    Your kind
letter of the 16th inst has just
been received and at this I
have not time to reply
as I could desire to do. I
must not lay it aside
without an acknowledgment.
        I have not seen Mr
Webster since the occasion

Continued on next page.

to which you refer. Tho I have thought of him often (particularly during this illness from which I trust he is now recovering) and never without profound admiration, gratitude for his kindness to me on many occasions, and a deep interest in everything connected with his happiness—

With thanks for your kind wishes, I am, Dr Sir.

Very truly

Yr Friend & Servt

Frank Pierce

Charles Lanman Esq

Washington

D.C.

FRANKLIN PIERCE, writing during his election campaign, pays eloquent tribute to Daniel Webster, who died shortly thereafter.

Wheatland, near Lancaster 7 April 1851

My dear Harriet /

Supposing that you are now in Baltimore, I send you the enclosed letter received yesterday. It was inadvertently opened by me; but the moment I saw it was addressed to "my dear Harriette", it was closed. It may contain love or treason for aught I know;

Eshredge was here yesterday; but he gave me no news, except that Mary & he were at a party at Mr McElrath on Wednesday evening last.

The place now begins to look beautiful & we have concerts of the birds every morning.. Stile I fear it will appear dull to you after your winters gaieties. Lewis has gone & we have a new coachman in the person of Mr. Frances Quinn who with his lady occupy the gardener's house. They have no children. Mr. Emanuel C Reigart will leave here on Saturday next for the world's fair & a trip to the continent. Your ci-devant lover Mr Evans purposes to go likewise; but many persons think he will not get off, on account of the expense — Mr & Mrs. Gorder prove to be very agreeable neighbours. They are furnishing their house & filling up their ground with much taste & at considerable expense. With my kindest regards for Mr & Mrs. White & the young ladies, I remain yours affectionately

James Buchanan

Miss Harriet Lane. —

BUCHANAN writes to his niece, Harriet Lane, who served as his hostess when he was President. Note how Buchanan made a special effort to avoid writing on two pages. (Library of Congress)

presidential franks. Although a signed photograph of Fillmore would run into three figures, a routine ALS can be obtained for as little as $30.

In writing to members of his family, Fillmore

tended to drop his habitual reserve. In 1871, for instance, he wrote a letter to a nephew in which he discussed the prerequisites for success in politics:

I have your letter of the 7th and was very glad to hear of your health and prosperity. I hope you adhere to the resolution which you formed some time since of laying up some thing from your salary for a less prosperous time. You must recollect that all political, and especially partisan favors, are very uncertain, and can not be relied upon for a permanent livelihood, and you should endeavor as far as possible to render yourself independent of them.

I note what you say of Genl. Strickland. . . . He seems to be a very active go-a-head fellow, and he may as you say overestimate himself, but it is difficult to say whether bold assurance or retiring modesty is most likely to succeed; probably a happy modicum of self reliance is best.[29]

Of all the "forgotten men" who have occupied the White House, perhaps none has generated more widespread amnesia than has Franklin Pierce. He remains the darkest horse ever nominated for the presidency; his nomination by a deadlocked Democratic convention in 1852 prompted one dumfounded observer to remark that "now no one is safe" from his party's call. Although Pierce had never been a national figure, he was "available" in 1852 after the Democratic front-runners had knocked one another out of contention. His main distinction as President was that he became the only one to date to maintain his cabinet intact for an entire administration.

Pierce's letters are no better than average in content, and, except for those as President, are readily obtainable. His handwriting is quite distinctive; the letters are frequently disconnected, and the reader is conscious of the preponderance of his downward strokes. At various times he signed himself Franklin, Fr., or Frank, generally reserving the last-named for close friends. Although Pierce's letters are common, his franks are not, certainly not by comparison to Fillmore and Buchanan. Among his presidential documents, generally most desirable are those military commissions countersigned by Jefferson Davis as Secretary of War. These generally cost at least $75, and at that figure are nearly double the price of a routine Pierce ALS.

Although not a scintillating correspondent, Pierce could be eloquent on occasion, and during the Civil War he was an outspoken critic of Lincoln for those actions which tended to circumscribe civil liberties in the North. Actually, Pierce had a gracious turn of phrase, and as with Fillmore, certain of his letters make up in style what they lack in content.

The third, and perhaps the most maligned, of the three presidents who preceded Lincoln was James Buchanan. A bachelor, Buchanan was a self-styled Old Public Functionary who spent the better part of his adult life in pursuit of the Democratic presidential nomination. It is ironic that, after he had capably discharged a variety of lesser posts, Buchanan found himself in the White House at the very time when the Union which he revered was beginning to collapse about him. Inevitably, his administration has been judged almost entirely in terms of its disastrous final year, as Buchanan strove ineffectually to reconcile his strict construction of the Executive's power with the growing threat of secession.

Buchanan was a prolific and often interesting correspondent. Although many of his letters relate to routine patronage matters, he did not hesitate to take pen in hand concerning the great questions of his day. Buchanan wrote in a small, attractive script. His letters are notable for their straight lines and attractive spacing. Like so many of his predecessors, he employed an oversized signature, which changed little in his lifetime.

Though his reputation has been in eclipse, Buchanan's autograph has always been in demand. It is required not only for presidential sets, but also for those of the Secretaries of State, to say nothing of collections centering on the Civil War. This demand notwithstanding, Buchanan's letters are fairly common. He is somewhat scarce in presidential ALS, but other ALS are common. While presidential documents of Buchanan are similarly plentiful, his LS are scarce except for those dating from his period as Secretary of State. In this connection, Buchanan brought to a close one early political tradition, that of the Department of State serving as a training ground for the presidency. Not since Buchanan has any incumbent or former Secretary of State reached the White House.

It was while Buchanan was Minister to Great Britain, awaiting the summons of his party, that he received a letter from the son of a friend, seeking advice before departing on a trip to Europe. Buchanan's response, written in January 1856, reflected his dedication to the ideals of the Constitution, as well as his difficulty in relating it to the growing agitation over slavery. He wrote in part,

I rejoice that you are pleased with the Free Academy.... You ought to aim at excellence—at superiority even over the good sheep: & this I am happy to believe is your determination. What a blessing it is to be the citizen of a country where each individual may proudly feel that he is equal to his fellow man & where merit is not eclipsed by birth & rank! Your visit to Europe will cause you to appreciate your happy lot as it deserves, & make you a more devoted republican than if you had never witnessed the working of monarchical government.

You pride yourself on being a true Democrat and this is well. Take care that throughout your life you shall never abandon the true political faith for any temporary advantage.... Do your duty and bide your time. It will surely come at last. Beware of any party not founded on the true principles of the Constitution & the Union.[30]

An early legal brief of ABRAHAM LINCOLN. Although the writing is smoother than Lincoln's later hand, certain characteristics, such as the hooked w's and n's, are already apparent. (Library of Congress)

CHAPTER TEN

A. Lincoln

SO MUCH HAS BEEN WRITTEN concerning the writings of Abraham Lincoln, including his famous letters, that it is difficult to do justice to his correspondence in a work of this scope. Certain of his letters, such as those to Horace Greeley and to the Workingmen of Manchester, England, rank among his major state papers. A number of his executive orders, particularly those which touch on the emancipation of the Negro, are milestones in Western civilization. The literary eloquence which Lincoln brought to the White House contributed mightily to the Lincoln legend as we know it today.

Along with Washington and Jefferson, Lincoln is the most sought-after of presidential autographs. As is the case with his distinguished predecessors, Lincoln's is not a truly scarce autograph. The current high prices are simply the result of heavy demand. Lincoln autographs are prized not only by Americans, but by many collectors abroad. Not long ago, a military commission of the type which Lincoln signed in large numbers could be obtained for around $100. The going rate is now over $300, and can be expected to continue upward as more and more Lincoln material disappears into institutions.

Many people have a favorite Lincoln letter among the many famous ones which he wrote. One of my favorites is a formal communication, a diplomatic letter in which he went far toward spelling out the substance of the Gettysburg Address. In the Spring of 1861, Lincoln received a letter from the Regent Captains of San Marino, the tiny republic located in the mountains between France and Italy. In reply Lincoln thanked them for the honorary citizenship they had conferred on him, and went on to observe,

> Although your dominion is small, your state is nevertheless one of the most honored in all history. It has by its experience demonstrated the truth, so full of encouragement to the friends of humanity, that government founded on republican principles is capable of being so administered as to be secure and enduring.
>
> You have kindly adverted to the trial through which this Republic is now passing. It is one of deep import. It involves the question whether a representative republic, extended and aggrandized so much as to be safe against foreign enemies, can save itself from the dangers of domestic faction. I have faith in a good result.
>
> Wishing that your interesting State may endure and flourish forever, and that you may live long and enjoy the confidence and secure the gratitude of your fellow citizens, I pray God to have you in his holy keeping.[31]

As far as the availability of Lincoln autographs is concerned, presidential letters and documents of Lincoln appear to be cataloged a good deal more frequently than material of pre-presidential date. This is not surprising, since Lincoln came into prominence comparatively late in his career, and there was little incentive for his respondents to preserve his earlier letters. The pre-presidential Lincoln is sometimes encountered in the form of legal briefs, usually on blue quarto sheets, signed in the name of one of the law firms with which he was associated: Stuart and Lincoln, Logan and Lincoln, and the most celebrated, Lincoln and Herndon. Envelopes and covers franked by Lincoln command high prices from philatelists. He had the franking privilege not only as President but also as Postmaster of New Salem (1833–1836) and as Congressman from Illinois (1847–1849).

There exist a number of remarkable autographs dating from Lincoln's pre-presidential period, in addition to the patent referred to earlier. One of these is the manuscript of one of Lincoln's longest but least-known addresses, a scientific lecture delivered in 1859 on "Discoveries, Inventions and Improvements." Following the Lincoln-Douglas debates, Lincoln obtained 100 bound copies of the debates which first brought him into national prominence. Some 25 of these are known to have been inscribed by Lincoln to various friends and colleagues.

Most of Lincoln's pre-presidential letters were written on the same quarto sheets which he favored for legal briefs. Although Lincoln was never verbose, his early letters tend to run longer than those of the presidential period, a reflection not only of the fact that he was under greater pressure once in the Executive Mansion, but perhaps of the fact that the standard letter size had not yet shrunk. Formal "Executive Mansion" stationery, first introduced by Lincoln, was half the size of his earlier quartos and provided one more incentive to brevity.

In the years of his presidency, Lincoln, like his predecessors, signed a seemingly endless stream of routine documents, including commissions for officers in the Union forces. He was the last President to be required to sign ships' papers, but continued to do so as long as the North had a merchant fleet able to put to sea. Occasionally, as with William Henry Harrison, a Lincoln ship's paper appears which was dated after his death![32] Official documents are almost the only autographs in which Lincoln's name appears in full. On less formal occasions, and for virtually all his correspondence, he preferred the abbreviated "A. Lincoln."

Apart from routine documents, Lincoln's presidential autograph is most frequently encountered in the form of endorsements on the numerous letters and petitions which crossed his desk. His leniency in cases involving disciplinary offenses by soldiers is legendary: "Let this man take the oath of allegiance and be discharged." Anyone other than a veteran collector, however, should be wary of Lincoln endorsements. Lincoln has always been a favorite subject for forgers, and several appear to have regarded his rugged, irregular hand as more susceptible to imitation than the more flowing script of a Washington or a Franklin. Two other factors make the detection of Lincoln forgeries more difficult: the relative abundance of authentic Civil War letters, to which the President might have had some reason to affix a note; and Lincoln's tendency to make repeated use of certain stock endorsements, e.g. "Respectfully submitted to the Sec. of War."

No mention of Lincoln would be complete without some comment on the use which he made of his correspondence while president. Although Lincoln was an accomplished stump speaker, circumstances permitted him to make comparatively few speeches while president. He thus relied to a considerable extent on letters and official papers to carry his views to the people, and no president has been more effective than he in this area. The United States was a sufficiently small country in 1865 that by the time of Lincoln's death millions of his countrymen felt that they knew him through word of mouth and the written word.

Lincoln's presidency coincided with a period of improving communications, notably the telegraph, and the rising circulation of newspapers. Yet Lincoln still made use of the personal letter, sometimes published, sometimes not, as a means of reaching the people. At the time of his election, Lincoln was less well-known than several members of his Cabinet. Lincoln corrected this situation in part through a stream of letters in which he elaborated his war aims, prodded recalcitrant generals, and gave expression to his own humor and compassion.

No better example of this could be given than Lincoln's famous letter to Mrs. Bixby, all of whose sons were believed in November 1864 to have died on the battlefield:

The phraseology of the Bixby letter is so char-

> Executive Mansion,
>
> Washington, January 31. 1862.
>
> Hon. Sec. of War
>
> My dear Sir:
>
> It is my wish that the expedition commonly called the "Lane Expedition" shall be as much as has been promised at the Adjutant General's Office, under the supervision of Gen. McClellan, and not any more. I have not intended, and do not now intend that it shall be a great exhausting affair; but a snug, sober column of 10.000 or 15.000— Gen. Lane has been told by me many times that he is under the command of Gen. Hunter, and assented to it as often as told. It was the distinct agreement between him & me when I appointed him, that he was to be under Hunter.
>
> Yours truly
>
> A. Lincoln

"... A snug, sober column of 10,000 or 15,000." An interesting reflection of Lincoln's early efforts to direct the war. (Library of Congress)

I have been shown in the files of the War Department a statement of the Adjutant General of Massachusetts, that you are the mother of five sons who have died gloriously on the field of battle.

I feel how weak and fruitless must be any words of mine which should attempt to beguile you from the grief of a loss so overwhelming. But I cannot refrain from tending to you the consolation that may be found in the thanks of the Republic they died to save.

I pray that our Heavenly Father may assuage the anguish of your bereavement, and leave you only the cherished memory of the loved and lost, and the solemn pride that

Gentlemen.

      In response to your address, allow me to attest the accuracy of its historical statements; indorse the sentiments it expresses; and thank you, in the nations name, for the sure promise it gives.

      Nobly sustained as the government has been by all the churches, I would utter nothing which might, in the least, appear invidious against any. Yet, without this, it may fairly be said that the Methodist Episcopal Church, not less devoted than the best, is, by its greater numbers, the most important of all. It is no fault in others that the Methodist Church sends more soldiers to the field, more nurses to the hospital, and more prayers to Heaven than any. God bless the Methodist Church — bless all the churches — and blessed be God, Who, in this our great trial, giveth us the churches.

A. Lincoln

May. 18. 1864

A LINCOLN speech text. Note that the writing is larger than in a typical letter. (Library of Congress)

must be yours, to have laid so costly a sacrifice upon the altar of Freedom. Yours, very sincerely and respectfully, A. Lincoln.[33]

acteristic of Lincoln that few have questioned that he actually wrote the letter. The original letter, however, has never been found. The situation has been confused by the appearance of facsimiles which purport to be copies of the original. These latter are not even true facsimiles, in that they are copies of a forgery. This is a point worth remembering while browsing in old antique shops.

Among the most historic of Lincoln autographs are the three original copies of the Thirteenth Amendment, by which slavery was abolished in the United States on February 1, 1865. Three copies were made, one each for the President, the Vice President, and the Speaker of the House. One of these is in the Huntington Library, and the second was recently sold at auction. The third copy has never been located, and, as with the Bixby letter, prospects for its recovery cannot be considered bright. As for the Gettysburg Address, there are at least five copies extant, all in Lincoln's hand. Three represent various stages in the drafting process, while two were written out by special request after the speech was delivered. None of the five is today in a private collection.

Because so many of Lincoln's important autographs have found their way into institutions, it is perhaps harder to obtain a letter of Lincoln with really fine content than one of any other president. Probably the most desirable Lincoln tiem to be sold in many years was the letter which he wrote as a presidential candidate to the little girl who had written that he would look more dignified with a beard. The letter was sold at auction in 1966 for $20,000 —the highest price ever paid for a Lincoln letter.

With all due deference for Lincoln's gracious reply (". . . As to the whiskers, never having worn any, do you not think people would call it a piece of silly affectation if I were to begin it now?"), the author feels that far too little attention has been accorded Miss Bedell's letter to Lincoln, which is here quoted in full:

N Y

Hon A B Lincoln   Westfield Chatauque Co
Dear Sir   Oct 15 1860
My father has just home from the fair and brought home your picture and Mr. Hamlin's. I am a little girl only eleven years old, but want you should be President of the United States very much so I hope you wont think me very bold to write to such a great man as you are. Have you any little girls about as large as I am if so give them my love and tell her to write me if you cannot answer this letter. I have got 4 brother's and part of them will vote for you any way and if you will let your whiskers grow I will try and get the rest of them to vote for you. you would look a great deal better for your face is so thin. All the ladies like whiskers and they would tease their husband's to vote for you and then you would be President. My father is going to vote for you and if I was a man I would vote for you but I will try and get every one to vote for you that I can. I think that rail fence around your picture makes it look very pretty. I have got a little baby sister she is nine weeks old and is just as cunning as can be. When you direct your letter dirct to Grace Bedell Westfield Chatauque County New York.

I must not write any more. answer this letter right off. Goodbye

Grace Bedell[34]

Speech of the Hon Andrew Johnson of Ten— —nessee on the President's message will be printed at the Globe Office @ $2.00 per hundred copies.

Names	Copies	Names	Copies
Andrew Johnson	10.000		100
William H. Seward	5.000	Z. Chandler, pen J.	200
Charles Sumner	500	J. R. Doolittle	100.
	450	L. Trumbull	100
	100	Dan Clark	100
H B Anthony	100	J F Porter	100
	200	Preston King	100

26,550

Commissions, $13.24

Mr Kennedy of the census sent wants 10,000 and the account sent to him A. Johnson

ANDREW JOHNSON orders 10,000 copies of a speech he delivered in the Senate, abbreviating his signature in the note at the bottom. (Library of Congress)

CHAPTER ELEVEN

The Gilded Age

GREAT PRESIDENTS have seldom come in bunches, nor did they in the period after Lincoln. Of the three presidents who followed the Great Emancipator, only Hayes left the White House with his reputation intact. Andrew Johnson proved to be inept as well as unpopular, while Grant, who had the greatest distance to fall in public esteem, largely dissipated in political life the reputation won on the battlefield. Only Hayes, whose background was the most pedestrian of the three, enhanced his stature in the eyes of his countrymen.

Johnson, who saw himself as the spiritual descendant of his fellow-Tennessean, Andrew Jackson, was the first American president whose background was neither legal nor military. The luminaries of the Virginia Dynasty, though basically large landowners, could point to an early bout with either the law or the military. Johnson's first trade had been that of a tailor, and he never forgot it. He was prone to remark on the humble origins of the Lincoln-Johnson ticket of 1864. Johnson, like Lincoln, was a self-made man, though unlike Lincoln he owed a great educational debt to his wife. Johnson never attended school, and was barely literate when he married his wife Eliza at the age of 17. For much of his early married life his wife assisted him in obtaining a rudimentary education.

Johnson's autographs to some degree reflect his limited schooling. Like Madison and the early Harrison, his autograph is plentiful in docu-mentary form, but his letters are somewhat scarce. One reason is evident from the letters themselves: his writing is labored, and it is evident from the content that Johnson got little pleasure from correspondence. This did not inhibit him once he got started, however, and his letters often ramble on for several pages.

Critical to any discussion of Johnson's presidential autograph is an injury he suffered to his arm shortly after entering the White House. As a result of this injury Johnson stopped signing military commissions entirely, and employed the first rubber stamp signature to find its way into the White House. Although the stamped signature is found on other documents as well as commissions, Johnson continued to sign warrants and pardons personally.

Except for his documents, Johnson is one of the scarcer Presidents. His ALS as President are extremely rare, presumably as a result of his injury, and a good example would probably run at least $500. Other ALS, of any length, cost from around $125 up. If Johnson does not stand out in terms of the content of his letters, neither was he a dull correspondent. Conscious of his humble beginnings, Johnson in politics inveighed alike against the wealthy slaveholder and the Yankee plutocrat. Those of Johnson's meatier letters often reflect his deep-seated prejudices. These prejudices contributed to his undoing, as Johnson sought unsuccessfully to turn over political power in the South to the yeoman class

Executive Mansion.

Washington, D.C. January 13ᵗʰ 1866.

Dear Sir:

I have received, through the Honᵇˡᵉ Mᵣ Radford, a copy of the 1ˢᵗ Volume of the "Fœderalist," edited by yourself, and also two numbers of your "Gleanings from the Harvest Field of American History." For these valuable publications I beg you to accept my thanks, with the assurance that I shall examine them with peculiar interest — especially your carefully prepared and elegantly printed edition of the "Fœderalist."

Very respectfully yours,

Andrew Johnson

*Henry B. Dawson Esq
Morrisania,
New York.*

A JOHNSON LS as President. (Library of Congress)

General GRANT in this note to Admiral Porter assists a Union man in recovering his property.

from which he had sprung, only in the process to return power to the same Bourbon elements which had fathered the Confederacy.

Johnson left the White House under a cloud, with memories of his narrow escape from impeachment still fresh. He was succeeded by Ulysses S. Grant, whose political activities during Johnson's term of office had so infuriated the President that Johnson followed John Quincy Adams' example in refusing to attend the inauguration of his successor.

Although Grant was in many respects a classic "simple soldier," his *Memoirs* clearly demonstrate that as a narrative writer he could stand comparison with most of our presidents. He had, moreover, one of the most attractive handwritings of any. While his signature varied in size somewhat over the years, predictably reaching its zenith while Grant was in the White House, the style of his writing, slanted and flowing, changed little throughout his life.

Appreciation of Grant as a letter writer has been slow in coming. Although demand for his letters has always been fairly high, coming as it has from Civil War as well as White House buffs, appreciation has lagged as a result of the abundance of his letters, together with the image

Final pages from an ALS in which GRANT describes a relaxed presidential summer.

of Grant as a plodding general and an inept president. Not only did Grant write a considerable number of very interesting letters, but even his more routine ones often embody a graceful turn of phrase. Although Grant occasionally wrote long letters, particularly during the Civil War, these were long of necessity and not from verbosity. All his life Grant seems to have handled his own correspondence; even during the war, when the demands on his time were greatest, almost all of his letters and orders came from his own hand.

Under the heading of incidental intelligence comes the fact that Grant was the first president to change his name from that on his birth certificate. He was born Hiram Ulysses Grant, but at the time of his entry into West Point he was mistakenly listed as Ulysses S. Grant, and the name stuck. I know of no Grant letter signed "Hiram" in his youth, but such letters could well exist. As such, they would be a major autographic curiosity.

Grant's autograph is plentiful in every form. Because of his key wartime role, Grant's wartime letters tend to be more interesting as a group than those of any other period, and as a result are probably more sought after even than those of presidential date. The latter most often deal with invitations and political appointments, and those with dramatic content are rare indeed. A fairly good ALS of Civil War date will run upward of $200. On the other hand, a routine presidential ALS can be found for considerably less.

One type of autograph variant in which Grant

<u>Private</u>

EXECUTIVE MANSION,
WASHINGTON.

7 Jany 1880

My Dear Colonel:

I have your note of the 5th inst. and in reply beg to assure you that I will give me great pleasure to put your name on the list referred to, without the formality of testimonials.

Sincerely

Col Emmons Clark

R B Hayes

A HAYES ALS in his characteristic crabbed handwriting.

EXECUTIVE MANSION
WASHINGTON.

26 Dec 1880

My Dear Sir:

I thank you heartily for the superb Christmas gift you have sent me. The tour of Gen Grant around the world, with its attendant circumstances, is one of the most wonderful events of our time. You have told the story of it admirably. I am particularly gratified to have from you so fine a copy of the great work.

With best wishes and the compliments of the season I am —

Sincerely
R B Hayes

Mr John Russell Young
&c &c

President HAYES makes a generous reference to his political rival, Grant. (Library of Congress)

is well represented is the signed *carte de visite* photograph. In the late 1850's, encouraged by the boom in camera portraits, there began a fad in which celebrities distributed 2″ × 4″ photos as visiting cards. These were sometimes signed, particularly if the visitor was unknown to the recipient. Such *cartes de visite* were the first signed presidential photos, and Grant signed these often prior to his presidential term, usually including his military rank. The fad passed almost as quickly as it began, but signed carte photographs can be obtained of Fillmore, Buchanan, Lincoln, Johnson, Grant, Hayes, and Garfield. The first four are scarce in such photos; the last three, including Grant, are not.

The third president to span the Gilded Age was perhaps least representative of it. Rutherford B. Hayes was a conscientious and dedicated public servant who, by a curious twist, was the target throughout his administration of charges that he had been fraudulently elected to office. It was characteristic of Hayes that he never questioned his party's contention that he was legally elected in the stormy election of 1876, notwithstanding a considerable body of evidence to the contrary.

It is curious that the victor in the most controversial American election should have been the unassuming Hayes. He had been wounded in the course of honorable service as a Union officer in the Civil War, and subsequently had served two terms as Governor of Ohio. His election as President, following as it did Grant's two victorious campaigns, set a pattern under which the Republicans regularly turned to former generals for their presidential candidates.

Hayes' autograph, like that of Grant, is one of the more common of the presidential series. There seems to be an endless supply of Hayes documents, particularly warrants. He is well represented in non-presidential documents too, having been not only a state govenor but also having been associated as an officer with various veterans' and other organizations.

Hayes' letters used to be as common as his documents, and at one time a Hayes ALS could be had for as little as five or ten dollars. Recently, the Hayes Library in Ohio has absorbed a great many of his letters, and prices have risen accordingly. There is something of a hen-scratching about Hayes' handwriting. His letters are always legible, but by no means pleasing to the eye. In terms of content, Hayes wrote rather uninteresting letters, though there are exceptions. In one presidential letter he wrote, "Nobody ever left the Presidency with less regret, less disappointment, fewer heartburnings, or more general content with the result of his term . . . than I do."

Like the Adamses and James K. Polk, Hayes kept a diary. One entry in 1846, provides a useful reminder that beneath the tightly buttoned waistcoat of a future statesman may beat the heart of a poet:

December 23, 1846— . . . What a world of time and brains are wasted in idle daydreams, castle-building visions of happiness too rapturous for reality. Am I in love, that it grows on me, or is it habit rising unchecked? . . . If in love, where's the sweetheart? Is it the noble-hearted F—? . . . The settled object is wanting. It is useless to attempt to cast myself free from the cords which a too warm imagination throws about me. The only cure is marriage. If that is not the specific, I may as well despair of ever making a respectable figure in life. . . .[35]

Hayes was responsible for one autograph innovation that holds considerable appeal for some collectors. During his presidential term, he inaugurated the practice of complying with autograph requests on an attractive card with "Executive Mansion" engraved at the top. These cards have continued to the present day, though with the engraving changed to "The White House" during the term of the first Roosevelt. Such cards are easily obtained for Hayes, Cleveland, and Coolidge. Those of the others are somewhat scarcer, and those of Garfield and Kennedy probably unobtainable. Because of the gap posed by the unavailability of these two presidents, and because the series goes back only to Hayes, White House cards of themselves do not make a very satisfying collection.

Dear Mr. Hoover:

We are starting a collection of autographs. If you could possibly spare the time, would you please send us your real signature. We would prefer this to a photostatic copy.

Our collection of autographs is just a hobby.

Hoover replied,

My dear Bonnie:

I can understand your preference for genuine autographs rather than photostats. This is genuine.

I was delighted to see that you are not a professional autograph hunter. Once upon a time one of those asked me for three autographs. I inquired why. He said, "It takes two of yours to get one of Babe Ruth's."[55]

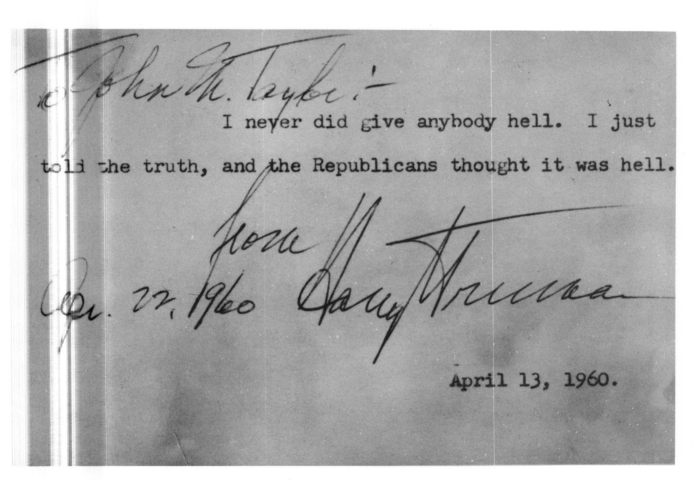

To John M. Taylor:—
I never did give anybody hell. I just told the truth, and the Republicans thought it was hell.

from
Apr. 27, 1960
Harry Truman

April 13, 1960.

Ex-President TRUMAN analyses an erroneous characterization of his speeches.

THE WHITE HOUSE
WASHINGTON

July 15, 1942

Dear George:

I thank you for your kindness in sending me yo
exchange of correspondence with the Foreign Ministe
at the time of Mexico's declaration of war.

It is very gratifying and encouraging to know
that such men as General Avila Camacho and Licencia
Padilla are guiding the destinies of Mexico in the
present emergency. They have shown themselves stat
men of the first order, men gifted with deep understanding and great wisdom.

I concur in your decision to remain at your po
for the time being. With Mexico's declaration of v
the two countries should move into a new stage of c
laboration--political, economic, and military. I
would feel much happier were you to be in Mexico wh
we are in this transitional stage. Your close per
friendships with the President and the Foreign Mini
together with the grasp which you have already show
of Mexican problems, will help us in moving forward
into our new war relationship with the maximum of
rapidity and success.

I am glad to learn that you have been able to
commodate yourself in a rather short period to the
conditions in Mexico, particularly to the altitude,
and I extend my best wishes for your continued suce
at your important post.

Very sincerely yours,

Franklin D Roosevelt

The Honorable
George S. Messersmith,
American Ambassador,
México, D. F.

A war letter from FRANKLIN D. ROOSEVELT to one of his ambassadors.

CHAPTER SEVENTEEN

The New Deal and After

FRANKLIN D. ROOSEVELT enjoys one notable distinction among American presidential autographs. He is the only president whose autograph I have never seen described in advertisements as "scarce as president."

In his three-plus terms in the White House, F.D.R. proved himself a master of speechmaking. His fireside chats made use of radio in a way which none of his predecessors had, though by the time Truman succeeded him such use of radio had been made obsolescent by the advent of TV. In his three terms, Roosevelt carried to its conclusion a trend which had been evident for some time: that of discarding the written word as a vehicle for major policy statements in favor of the public address. Among our early presidents, correspondence was the primary means for the exchange of ideas. As recently as the administrations of Theodore Roosevelt and Wilson, the "public" letter—designed to be passed around, or even released to the press, by the recipient—was an accepted means of setting the president's views on record. But radio put an end to all this. Although Bartlett's *Familiar Quotations* devotes more than four pages to notable quotations by F.D.R., not one of these is derived from a letter.

It is therefore hardly surprising that Roosevelt's letters tend to be routine in content. This is ironic, for while F.D.R.'s autograph collecting has been overshadowed by his well-known interest in philately, he was the only president prior to John F. Kennedy who could be characterized as himself an autograph collector.

Charles Hamilton, in his book on collecting, quotes a note from Roosevelt to a collector in which the future president noted, "I too collect autographic letters but for historical reasons."[56]

Like all recent presidents F.D.R. is scarce in ALS, although not nearly so rare as Hoover, Truman or Eisenhower. Such holograph examples as turn up are almost invariably of pre-presidential date, usually in the period between Roosevelt's service as Wilson's Assistant Secretary of the Navy and his election as Governor of New York. I do not recall having seen a presidential ALS of F.D.R.

In his early government service in Washington, Roosevelt was prone to sign letters F. D. Roosevelt, much as Hoover at one stage used his first two initials. Once Governor of New York, Roosevelt began writing out his first name in full, though he was not above grumbling at the time required to write his full signature. To intimates he frequently signed letters with his famous initials.

Roosevelt as President favored a thick-stub pen and India ink, a combination which caused some of his signatures to look as if they were facsimiles. Under examination, however, the shades and variations of the holograph signature are discernible. Although Roosevelt's signature underwent minor variations during his lifetime, not until the last year of his life was there a pronounced change. The contrast between the bold signature of Roosevelt's first two terms and the small, shaky writing of his final year in office is very marked.

statements in the report which have relation to the

possibility of bringing the convention and protocol into

force on January 1, 1945, in accordance with a provision

in Article 27 of the convention.

Franklin D Roosevelt

Enclosures:

    1. Report of the Acting
Secretary of State.

    2. Convention and protocol
of July 25, 1939, between
the United States and
France for the avoidance of
double taxation.

THE WHITE HOUSE,
November 30, 1944

Final page of a rare type of letter, transmitting data to the Senate. The small, shaky signature shown
acteristic of ROOSEVELT in the last months of his life.

THE WHITE HOUSE

WASHINGTON

October 11, 1946

Dear General Taylor:

I appreciated most highly the letter
from the Librarian, Colonel Morton,
enclosing copy of a statement by Jefferson
on Military Training.

I also appreciated very highly the bound
book of pictures of the visit to West
Point - they are most interesting and I
will be glad to keep them in my collection.

Everybody enjoyed the visit and the ball-
game very much.

Please express my regards to Mrs. Taylor
and my appreciation for all the courtesies
extended me while I was at West Point.

Sincerely yours,

Harry Truman

Major General Maxwell D. Taylor
Superintendent
United States Military Academy
West Point, New York

A TRUMAN LS with an unusually large signature.

Somewhat more of a problem than his India ink is the use Roosevelt made of proxy signatures in the period prior to his presidency. Charles Hamilton states that seven or more secretaries,

A scarce EISENHOWER holograph in which the future president sends congratulations to the Army following its famous scoreless tie with Notre Dame in 1946. (Author's collection)

at various times, were authorized to sign for Roosevelt. Most of the resulting proxy signatures are easily recognized as such, though all of his proxies appear to have made some attempt to imitate his handwriting. A couple of them achieved a level comparable to that of Coolidge's secretary, although none was as facile as Harding's senatorial assistant.

Considering his impact on history, there is remarkably little collector interest in Roosevelt. Two reasons already cited are the availability of Roosevelt letters and the scarcity of letters of good content. Along with Grover Cleveland, he is one of the few of the "important" presidents who can still be collected in some depth without driving the collector to bankrupcy.

The autograph of Harry S. Truman, along with that of Hoover, is probably the most common of all presidential autographs. Like Hoover, Truman spent several decades in public life, carrying on an extensive correspondence before, during, and after his presidency. Unlike Hoover, who flirted briefly with a facsimile signature, Truman appears to have signed every letter that went out in his name. Like his predecessor, Truman favored a dark ink that at times causes his signature to resemble a facsimile.

In contrast to his immediate predecessors, who were nothing if not cautious correspondents, Truman wrote a good letter. Many readers will recall Truman's famous letter, a presidential ALS, by the way, to the music critic who had had harsh words for a concert by Margaret Truman. "I never met you," the irate President wrote, "but if I do you'll need a new nose and plenty of beefsteak." This remains by all odds the most fascinating Truman letter of which I have knowledge. Several years ago it was sold by the critic to whom it was addressed, Paul Hume, to a private collector. During 1966 it was sold to a second collector for a price reportedly in the neighborhood of $3,500. This is by far the highest price ever paid for a Truman autograph.

Among Truman's most interesting letters are those written to his family while President, on which Mr. Truman drew extensively in writing

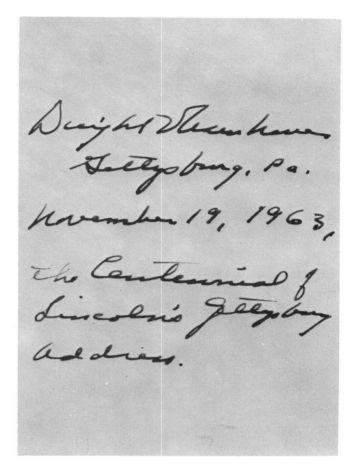

An unusual inscription by EISENHOWER on an album page.

his *Memoirs*. In them, Truman revealed himself as a warm, newsy correspondent—a fact that makes more curious his unwillingness to permit quotations from his *Memoirs*.

Probably no president, even Hoover, was more accommodating to collectors than was Truman prior to the broken hip which he suffered in 1964 and which forced him greatly to curtail his activities. Autograph catalogues abound with souvenir autographs provided by Truman, many of them quite interesting. These include signed copies of press conference transcripts and presidential proclamations; photos of a smiling Truman holding aloft a newspaper with the headline, "Dewey Defeats Truman;" and exerpts from various speeches. There are probably more inscribed photographs of Truman than of any other president. Almost invariably Truman dated items which he autographed subsequent to his presidency. Inscribed photographs which I have seen without any date show evidence of having been inscribed while president.

Truman's letters are inexpensive. A routine example as ex-president can be obtained for $10 or $15, and a White House LS for around $50. An ALS of even the most routine content, however, would bring at least $150. A great deal of Truman material can be expected to come onto the market in the next decade or so, as people with whom he corresponded clean out their files and dispose of his letters in one way or another. As a result, Truman is one of the few presidents whose autograph will probably not rise in price over the next few years.

A not-too-friendly critic of President Eisenhower, presumably a veteran of numerous Eisenhower press conferences, was moved to rewrite the Gettysburg Address as it might have been delivered by Ike. It began like this:

Whatever may be said of Eisenhower as an impromptu speaker, and much has indeed been said, the implication that Eisenhower was a malaprop thinker of the Harding mold does not square with the facts. The ability to speak well extemporaneously is granted to comparatively few people, and Ike was not among the chosen. Only occasionally, as when at Dartmouth College he importuned his listeners not to join "the bookburners," did he achieve a certain eloquence.

I haven't checked these figures but 87 years ago, I think it was, a number of individuals organized a governmental set-up here in this country, I believe it convered certain Eastern areas, with this idea they were following up based on a sort of national independence arrangement. . . .[57]

What, then, of Eisenhower as a correspondent? I can only recall seeing one Eisenhower letter of really dramatic content. In it, he detailed his admiration for Robert E. Lee as a soldier and a man, in reply to a critic who thought it inappropriate for Lee's picture to hang in the President's office. By and large, however, the Eisenhower letters which I have seen are not memorable for their content. They are, however, logical, grammatical and largely not susceptible to the type of criticism sometimes leveled at his speeches.

This would appear to be as g any to note that a penchant fo letters, so dear to the autograph not necessarily represent an asset much less qualify him for his h can argue that prior to the turn when the telephone had reduced of correspondence as a communic there was some correlation betw of historians and collectors conce teenth-century presidents. In regarded by historians as "great" were also respected by collectors of their correspondence. In this g certainly place Washington, Jeff Lincoln, and Cleveland.

It is not difficult to see why breaks down in recent decades. V ern presidents have had somethi to say, they have generally comn by telephone, telegraph, or perso the latter now facilitated by jet tr can bring an American ambassad ton from any part of the world With the written word now le the conduct of the Executive bra ment, the fact that the known lett X are regarded by collectors as inspired no longer gives a hint as

While Eisenhower was in the his letters were assiduously sou tors, as is usually the case with president. Since his retirement eased, partly because enough Eis were around to meet the dema because his successor emerged as modern presidents. White Ho Eisenhower are still moderately s can be expected to come onto increasing numbers. It goes with he is rare in ALS, and a full Ei should bring upward of $250.

Eisenhower usually signed his employing the middle initial a ill-defined "D" into the "E" of t friends and acquaintances, he wo use the initials "D.E.;" on rar employed the nickname by which he was known to millions and would sign himself "Ike E." Eisenhower presents relatively minor problems to the collector in terms of proxy signatures. He employed secretarial signatures briefly while campaigning for the presidency in 1952, but letters signed thus are only occasionally encountered. White House cards of Eisenhower are rare, however, in part because he had such cards prepared with a facsimile inscription and signature. The facsimile is easily recognized as such.

Eisenhower, like Hoover and Truman, was granted the franking privilege after leaving the White House. As have the others, Eisenhower has used a printed frank, and I do not recall ever having seen advertised a holograph frank of Eisenhower.

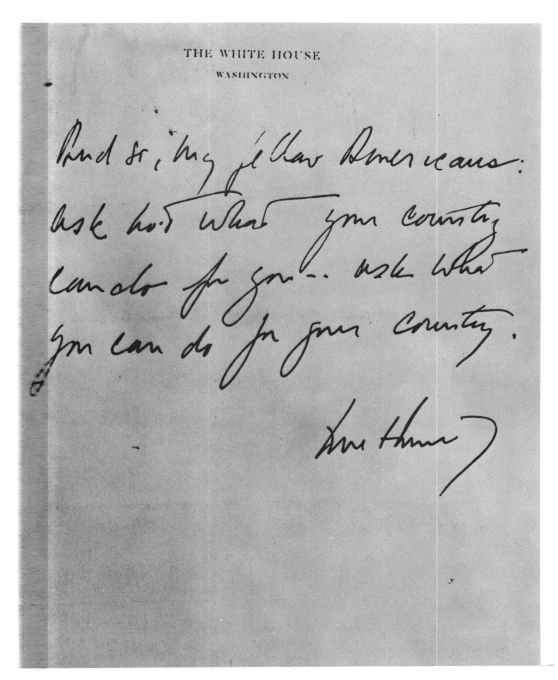

A transcription by President KENNEDY of an oft-quoted excerpt from his inaugural speech.

THE WHITE HOUSE

WASHINGTON

October 25, 1963

MEMORANDUM FOR

GENERAL TAYLOR

Tom Watson was in to see me today
in connection with the program of the
Business Advisory Council meeting to be
held on December 4th and 5th. They are
most anxious for you to speak to this
group on the 4th. If your schedule
permits I hope it will be possible for
you to be with them at that time as this
is a significant group.

General Taylor replied to President by dictating
note to Mrs. Lincoln over telephone:

"Mr. President:
With regard to your suggestion that I
address the Business Advisory Council on
December 4 & 5, I regret to say that under
present plans I shall be in the Far East. I
have informed Tom Watson and expressed
my regret."

An unusual form of KENNEDY LS. The underlining is that of the President.

CHAPTER EIGHTEEN

Kennedy and Johnson

For historians of the twentieth century, the problem [of sources] is compounded by the technological revolution—in particular, by the invention of the typewriter and the telephone. In the good old days, statesmen, quill pen in hand, could write only a limited number of letters. When they had something of significance to communicate, paper was the only means—save face-to-face conversation—of communication. In our time, the typewriter has vastly increased the flow of paper, while the telephone has vastly reduced its importance. Far more documents are produced —and there is far less in them. If a statesman in the twentieth century has something significant to communicate, if speed and secrecy are of the essence, he will confide his message not to a letter, but to the telephone. Electronic waves, alas, leave few traces.

ARTHUR M. SCHLESINGER, Jr., "The Historian and History," *Foreign Affairs,* April 1963, pp. 493–94.

IN THE PRECEDING CHAPTERS, I have noted where relevant the existence of forgeries which pose a threat to the unwary collector. In general, however, the commentary has centered on the various forms of presidential autographs, their relative scarcity, and the quality of a given president's letters. When one comes to Kennedy and Johnson, however, the terms of reference are changed. In the case of these two, all other considerations are subordinate to the question: Is the signature genuine?

Many individuals have had an impact on presidential autographs as we know them today. Hayes inaugurated the White House card, Arthur brought in the typewriter. But no one has had a greater impact than John F. Kennedy, who introduced the mechanical signature. Whereas the knowledgeable collector or dealer can recognize the facsimile signature, the forgery, or the rubber stamp, the robot signature is almost perfect. It is in fact too perfect, for whereas no person writes the identical signature twice, the robot does exactly that, thereby permitting the identification of "repeaters" as the product of the mechanical pen.

When John F. Kennedy entered the White House, there was no reason to believe that his would prove to be a scarce autograph, and every reason to believe that it would not. The President was young and was a prolific correspondent. Many collectors had already brought their collections up to date with a JFK example dating from his period as congressman or United States senator. By the time of the assassination, these earlier letters were coming under close scrutiny, and it became known that the great majority of his senatorial LS bore robot signatures. Moreover, there was abundant evidence that the great majority of books and photographs "inscribed" by the President were in fact inscribed by various secretaries, whose problems in attempting to imitate Kennedy's script were enough to arouse a certain sympathy.

Following the tragedy in Dallas, collectors awoke to the realization that the President whom they had assumed would prove so common in autographic form promised in fact to become one of the scarcest. This awareness, together with a surge of belated affection for the slain President, resulted in a demand for Kennedy autographs which at this writing has abated only slightly. Authenticated Kennedy LS, often routine in content, have recently brought more than

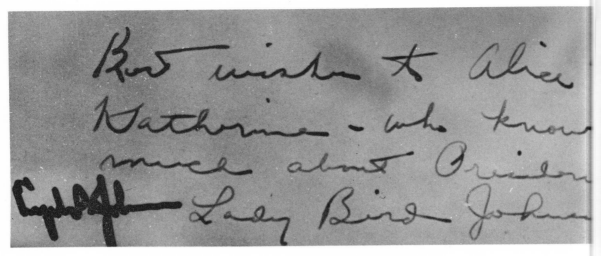

Signature of President and Lady Bird JOHNSON.

$300 at auction. A prominent New York dealer, in an attempt to separate the chaff from the wheat in terms of Kennedy autographs, has published a monograph devoted solely to autographs of the thirty-fifth president.[58] One may ask how long the Kennedy boom will last. While predictions are difficult, it appears likely that authentic Kennedy material will continue to come onto the market, and that prices will gradually drop to more rational levels.

Along with Franklin D. Roosevelt, Kennedy was himself a collector of autograph letters. In a letter written in 1955 the future president asked an antiquarian dealer that he be informed of new acquisitions, "particularly any old letters of historical interest." In 1961, on the occasion of his first meeting with President de Gaulle of France, Kennedy presented as his personal gift a letter from Lafayette to George Washington.

What, then, of Lyndon F. Johnson? Presidential collectors, many of whom were "burned" in connection with Kennedy letters, are understandably wary of Johnson letters currently in circulation. One well-known dealer has indicated that he will not handle Johnson autographs until more information is available with which to determine their authenticity. Existing suspicions tend to be confirmed by the remarkable variations in Johnson's signature. LBJ, like Kennedy, employed a signature as president which differed

considerably from his signature a[s] later as vice president.

A point which should be emph[] few dealers or collectors begrudge[] the benefit of any labor-saving [] can be made available to him. (In a[] not Lyndon but Andrew Johns[on] sought a mechanical aid for his sig[] The insidiousness of the robot sig[] ever, lies in its intent to deceive. A[] signature is recognizable as such; t[] signature generally is not.

In August 1966, while working[] I wrote a letter to presidential P[] Bill Moyers calling attention to[] which exists among collectors as [] widespread use of robot signatur[] knowledging that the number[] collectors was small by compariso[] of stamps and coins, I asked whet[] collectors could not be assisted to[] the White House's providing some[] statement concerning the types [] documents which are usually, some[] personally signed by the President.[] never acknowledged.

Apart from the key problem of a[] it is obviously difficult at this tim[] the quality of such Kennedy and J[] rial as is available to the public. I do[] whether either will be adjudged[] spondent. President Kennedy in p[]

THE WHITE HOUSE
WASHINGTON

July 8, 1965

Dear Max:

It is with great regret that I accept your resignation as Ambassador to the Republic of South Viet-Nam. I do so only because I am bound to honor the understanding we had at the time of your initial appointment.

You have served your country and the cause of freedom with extraordinary courage and skill throughout a long and brilliant career. There is no prouder page in that record than the one which you have written in the last year. Your determination to resist aggression and your imaginative understanding of the aspirations and the problems of the people and Government of Viet-Nam have made you an outstanding Ambassador in a critical year.

We shall miss you, but no man has more fully earned the right to meet his personal obligations. I am grateful for your offer of continued help as a private citizen, and you can be sure that I will value your counsel as long as I am President.

Sincerely,

Honorable Maxwell D. Taylor
American Ambassador
Saigon, Viet-Nam

An LS of President JOHNSON. Note the characteristic dot below the line.

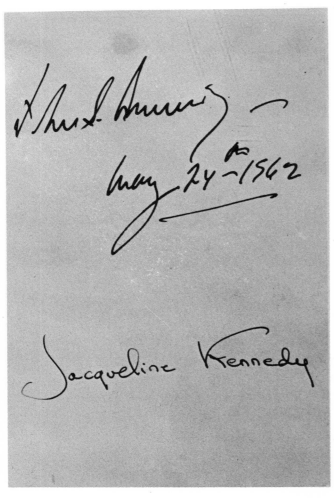

Signatures of President and Mrs. KENNEDY on an album page.

interest in the collection of historica:
To the general collector, the only ·
horizon is that of escalating prices. V
collecting autographs in the late 1ç
my first purchases were an inscrib
General Sherman for $1.50 and
ALS of Charles Sumner for $2.5c
prices are determined primarily
however, and the recent increase in
of collectors, together with the c·
sorption of material into institutio:
tably driven prices skyward.

There are a number of areas in v
tant collections can be developed
modest cost —for instance, Secreta
explorers, and foreign statesmen. TI
however, have led the rise in prices
decade or so. The upward trend i
tainly here to stay, and the bu
collector of the future will do well
than to presidential autographs.

There is another trend in recen
letters which may, in time, affe·
habits, and it is hinted at by Profeso:
at the beginning of this chapter. .
transact less and less important busi
their correspondence becomes incr
tine. Will collector interest co:
presidents no longer write "impo:
Probably it will, but the day may :
distant when even a discriminating
presidential letters will contain a hig
of routine acknowledgments.

But the White House will conti:
the interest of historians, scholars, ·
regardless of the standard of corre·
its occupants. Thus the trend in au:
be away from complete sets of t:
but in the direction of specializatic
individual, such as Monroe, Tyler,
Regardless of what collecting trends
interest in presidential autographs
as long as the presidency itself
children's shoes can wait.

stimulating writer, and some of his letters with the robot signature have fetched respectable prices at auction solely on the basis of their content.

It appears very likely that, unless LBJ is revealed to be using mechanical signatures almost exclusively, his is well on the way to becoming one of the more common presidential autographs. He will doubtless prove rare in ALS, as have all of his immediate predecessors. But he has a strong prediliction for inscribed photographs, and anyone visiting the White House on business is likely to receive a photograph of his meeting with the President, duly inscribed.

Despite the hazards noted in this chapter and elsewhere, I see no likelihood of a diminishing

Epilogue

Before I end my letter, I pray Heaven to bestow
the best of blessings on this house and all that
shall hereafter inhabit it. May none but wise and
honest men ever rule under this roof.

JOHN ADAMS TO ABIGAIL ADAMS

Executive Mansion
November 2, 1800

Presidential Signatures

NOT LONG AGO comparatively few dealers bothered to handle signatures unless they were unusual rarities. Today, with prices for autograph letters at an all-time high, and quality material scarce, the lowly signature is once again achieving a certain respectability. Why, the collector asks, should he spend in three figures for a presidential letter of no particular substance, when the same individual's signature may be obtained for a fraction of that sum? Why indeed.

Every autograph is unique. Even in the case of routine documents or signatures, no one signs his name in identical fashion twice in a row. As a result, even clipped signatures come in various shapes and variations, to say nothing of differences which derive from the type of ink employed, the quality of paper, and other factors. Yet if there is a yardstick by which to measure demand for autographs of the Presidents, the current price for presidential signatures represents one standard of comparison.

Prices for presidential signatures reflect the same law of supply and demand as do those of other presidential autographs. Thus, for the most part, signature prices noted below are consistent with their general autographic desirability as discussed in the preceding chapters. As with other forms of autographs, however, certain Presidents are frequently encountered in the signature form, and others much less frequently. Signatures of Washington, for instance, are rare; past genera-

tions appear to have treated his letters with more respect than that accorded other Chief Executives. Similarly, Presidents William Henry Harrison, Taylor, and Franklin Roosevelt are scarcer in signatures than in other forms, perhaps because none had the franking privilege for any significant period after reaching the White House.

The following are current prices for presidential signatures, in good condition, either removed from other pieces or on cards. They should not be confused with White House cards, which are a category apart and much more expensive.

Washington—$200	Grant—$12.50
John Adams—$65	Hayes—$10
Jefferson—$85	Garfield—$10
Madison—$25	Arthur—$12.50
Monroe—$15	Cleveland—$12.50
J. Q. Adams—$15	Benj. Harrison—$10
Jackson—$20	McKinley—$10
Van Buren—$12.50	T. Roosevelt—$10
W. H. Harrison—$25	Taft—$7.50
Tyler—$15	Wilson—$15
Polk—$30	Harding—$12.50
Taylor—$40	Coolidge—$10
Fillmore—$10	Hoover—$5
Pierce—$15	F. D. Roosevelt –$15
Buchanan—$12.50	Truman—$7.50
Lincoln—$165	Eisenhower—$10
Johnson—$12.50	Kennedy—$50
	L. B. Johnson—$15

Bibliographic Comment

ALTHOUGH THERE IS NOW a growing shelf of books on the subject of autographs, such books have heretofore been general treatises in which presidential autographs, where dealt with at all, have usually been accorded one chapter among many. This should not be construed as criticism, for there are almost as many collecting specialties as there are autograph collectors, and authors of earlier books—who with few exceptions have been dealers—have sought to interest the widest possible audience. Considering the specialized publications available in other hobby fields, however, it is somewhat surprising that to date no full volume has been devoted to collecting either Presidents or the Signers.

Of those books which include sections on the Presidents, I have long had a special regard for one by a famous dealer of the twenties and thirties, THOMAS F. MADIGAN. His *Word Shadows of the Great* (Frederick A. Stokes Company, New York, 1930) conveys much of the excitement of collecting, and deals quite fully with the Presidents. Not surprisingly, however, the appendix in which he discusses prices is far out of date.

The most recent and by far the best illustrated book on autographs is that of CHARLES HAMILTON, *Collecting Autographs and Manuscripts* (University of Oklahoma Press, Norman, 1961). Its more than 800 facsimiles and other reproductions make this a most useful reference, though a number of presidents are unmentioned except for a reproduction of their signature. Far more specialized is Mr. Hamilton's study of John F. Kennedy's use of a mechanical signature. Entitled *The Robot That Helped to Make a President,* it is a valuable reference as to the authenticity of Kennedy signatures, particularly those of pre-White House vintage.

Elsewhere, useful references are limited in number and often in quality. Two volumes of marginal interest are ROBERT WILLIAMS' *Adventures of an Autograph Collector* (Exposition Press, New York, 1952) and MARY A. BENJAMIN, *Autographs: A Key to Collecting* (R. R. Bowker Co., New York, 1946).

Notes

CHAPTER 1: PRESIDENT WASHINGTON

1. J. A. Carroll and M. W. Ashworth, *George Washington: First in Peace*, p. 135.
2. Douglas Southall Freeman, *Washington*, IV, p. 7.
3. Carroll and Ashworth, *op. cit.*, p. 312.
4. *Ibid.*, p. 287.

CHAPTER 3: THOMAS JEFFERSON

5. Adrienne Koch and William Peden, eds., *The Life and Selected Writings of Thomas Jefferson*, p. 435.
6. *Ibid.*, p. 27.
7. C. T. Harnsburger, ed., *Treasury of Presidential Quotations*, p. 53.

CHAPTER 4: THE TWO ADAMSES

8. Page Smith, *John Adams*, II, pp. 621–22. Quoted by permission of Doubleday and Co., Inc.
9. *Ibid.*, II, p. 890.
10. C. F. Adams, *Familiar Letters of John Adams and His Wife Abigail Adams During the Revolution*, p. 193.
11. Abigail Adams is on record concerning this point, having written that "There is nothing so much to render a man fractious as living without females about him. . . . They know how to temper the wind to the shorn lamb." Smith, *op. cit.*, II, p. 993.
12. Samuel F. Bemis, *John Quincy Adams and the Union*, p. 102.
13. Smith, *op. cit.*, II, p. 1137.
14. Bemis, *op. cit.*, p. 328.
15. Charles Francis Adams, Jr., *Autobiography*, p. 9.

CHAPTER 5: THE VIRGINIA DYNASTY

16. Madison to George Washington, June 21, 1792, Quoted in Harnsburger, *op. cit.*
17. J. A. Carroll and M. W. Ashworth, *George Washington: First in Peace*, p. 493.

18. Madison to Payne Madison, Nov. 13, 1825. Collection of Dr. Herbert Klingelhofer.
19. Monroe to David Gelston, February 7, 1809. Quoted in Harnsburger, *op. cit.*, p. 47.
20. Monroe to Thomas Jefferson, February 23, 1826. Jefferson Papers, Library of Congress.

CHAPTER 6: THE JACKSONIANS

21. Jackson to Gen. John Coffee, December 1832. Quoted in Harnsburger, *op. cit*, pp. 191–92.
22. Bemis, *op. cit.*, p. 250.
23. In addition to Van Buren, Pierce, Fillmore and Tyler were still living when the Civil War began, although only Fillmore survived it. Although only Tyler supported the Confederate cause, both Pierce and Fillmore were at times severely critical of the Lincoln administration.

CHAPTER 7: TIPPECANOE AND TYLER, TOO

24. Brainard Dyer, *Zachary Taylor*, p. 131.
25. Joseph N. Kane, *Facts About the Presidents*, p. 77.

CHAPTER 8: POLK AND TAYLOR

26. Ulysses S. Grant, *Personal Memoirs*, I, p. 139.
27. Brainard Dyer, *Zachary Taylor*, p. 271.
28. James K. Polk, *Diary*, IV, p. 261 (December 29, 1848). Huoted in Harnsburger, *op. cip*, p. 66.

CHAPTER 9: FORGOTTEN MEN

29. Fillmore to G. M. Fillmore, February 10, 1871. Author's collection.
30. Buchanan to Reed Sanders, January 25, 1856. Author's collection.

CHAPTER 10: A. LINCOLN

31. Roy Basler, ed., *The Collected Works of Abraham Lincoln,* IV, p. 360.

32. Following the Civil War, validation of port clearances was left to the Department of State, which removed an onerous burden from the President, but which closed the book on perhaps the most romantic of early presidential documents.

33. Basler, *op. cit.,* VIII, pp. 116–17.

34. *Ibid.,* IV, p. 130.

CHAPTER 11: THE GILDED AGE

35. Harry Barnard, *Rutherford B. Hayes and His America,* p. 155.

CHAPTER 12: GARFIELD AND ARTHUR

36. Garfield to S. P. Wollcott, April 13, 1874. Author's collection.

37. By a curious coincidence, the person named by Hayes to succeed Arthur was Theodore Roosevelt, Sr., father of the 26th President.

38. Arthur to D. F. Phelps, September 9, 1878. Author's collection.

CHAPTER 13: CLEVELAND AND HARRISON

39. Alistair Cooke, ed., *The Vintage Mencken,* pp. 216–17.

40. Nevertheless, Cleveland is probably given too much credit in connection with his 1884 campaign slogan, "A public office is a public trust." As recently as four years earlier, Garfield's Democratic opponent, General Winfield S. Hancock, had campaigned on the nearly identical slogan, "A public office is a trust."

41. Allan Nevins, *Grover Cleveland,* p. 563.

CHAPTER 14: THE AGE OF TEDDY

42. Margaret Leech, *In the Days of McKinley,* pp. 237–38.

43. William A. White, *Masks in a Pag*

44. William Allen White, *Autobiograp*

45. Herman Hagedorn, *The Roosevelt I* Hill, p. 176.

46. White, *op. cit.,* p. 545.

47. William H. Taft, *The Presidency,*

48. Henry F. Pringle, *The Life and* Howard Taft, II, p. 858.

CHAPTER 15: A STUDY IN CC WILSON & HARDIN

49. Eleanor Wilson McAdoo, "The Co row Wilson," *American Heritage,* Octobe

50. Gene Smith, *When the Cheering S* Years of Woodrow Wilson, p. 136.

51. Andrew Sinclair, *The Available M*

52. Harding to Col. and Mrs. Christian

CHAPTER 16: TWO FOR TH

53. Alistair Cooke, ed., *The Vintage M*

54. Herbert Hoover, *On Growing Up,*

55. *Ibid.,* p. 74.

CHAPTER 17: THE NEW DEAL

56. Charles Hamilton, *Collecting Auto* scripts, p. 6. Quoted by permission of t Oklahoma Press.

57. Oliver Jensen, "The Gettysburg *A* howese," quoted in Dwight Macdonald, Anthology, p. 447. Used by permission.

CHAPTER 18: KENNEDY AND

58. Charles Hamilton, *The Robot Tha* a President.

Index

Page numbers printed in italics refer to plates.